THE TATTER OF LIFE

By

LISA BARRON

tat·ter[1]
(tăt′ər) *n. 1.* A torn and hanging piece of cloth; a shred. tat/*verb* - make (a decorative mat or edging) by tying knots in thread and using a small shuttle to form lace
2. tat·ter[2] (tăt′ər) *n.* - One that makes lace, especially as a livelihood.

Dedicated to

Our Mother

Acknowledgements

I am deeply grateful for the generosity of Renae, Rita Foley, Rob Hutcheon, Danielle Kelleher, Sue Nickson, Robert and Radhika Richardson, Anil Sattarshetty, Angela, Carrie, Dan, Tina, Adele, Rajesh Bhasale, Angela, Priya and a couple of other very special people. Without them "The Tatter of Life" would never have become a book. It would have remained a pile of notebooks and diaries.

I also express deep gratitude for all the people that enriched my life during this unique time.

Needless to say huge thanks goes to Ralph Wessman of Burringbah Books for patiently answering all my questions and for creating this book.

Without my Mother's love nothing would have happened.

ISBN 9781877010842

Burringbah Books
PO Box 368
North Hobart
Tasmania 7002

March 2018

Introduction

Long before thoughts came, I felt whispers of an ancient feeling- a feeling of being a part of everywhere and everything but belonging to nothing. The desire to find the source of this elusive feeling overwhelmed me and forced my crippled legs to walk. I had to walk to find its source.

CONTENTS

Chapter 1	Landing	1
Chapter 2	The Lady on the Table	7
Chapter 3	Beyond the Horizon and the Other Side of Eyelids	13
Chapter 4	Plaster Prisons and Inner Retreats	23
Chapter 5	Lisa and That Little Word I	26
Chapter 6	Maths and Idealism	30
Chapter 7	Silver Commas, a Cross and Dreams	33
Chapter 8	The Lady on TV	39
Chapter 9	That Social God Called Alcohol and Sitting on the Rock	42
Chapter 10	Dropping Out	49
Chapter 11	Different Threads	52
Chapter 12	Gibbo, Rosary Beads and a Chain around My Neck	56
Chapter 13	Redhead to Redfern	62
Chapter 14	Wedded Bliss, Tanaya and Meeting My Hero	68
Chapter 15	Separation and the Worst Insult to Planet Earth	78
Chapter 16	The Earthquake and a Gnawing Feeling	89
Chapter 17	Finding That Feeling	98
Chapter 18	A Small Breeze and the Comforter	110
Chapter 19	Connecting to That Fourth Dimension	125
Chapter 20	Shri Mataji's Visit	128
Chapter 21	Muswellbrook and Miracles	134
Chapter 22	Finding the Reality of Dreams	143
Chapter 23	It Came Without Wrapping	155
Chapter 24	A Place of Patience	159
Chapter 25	A Curfew, A Sugar Cane Field and the Lap of the Himalayas	163
Chapter 26	There is Nothing, Separate So There is Nothing to Fear	168
Chapter 27	Riots and an Idyllic Existence	176
Chapter 28	Vashi, a Movie, Theatre and a Victory Ride	179
Chapter 29	A Ganapatapule Christmas with Mary and My True Self	184
	Epilogue	192

Chapter 1

Landing

I remember when I landed.

I remember it clearly. My eyes slowly opened. Before me was a white wall. My hand lay in front of me on a pillow.

"So this is my hand this time. It looks so different from before. I am here."

These thoughts slowly took form. They were the first thoughts to crystallize this time-this lifetime. I slowly rolled over in my new big bed. It felt like a giant cocoon similar to the dark one that I had journeyed to all of my destinations in.

A long hallway stretched beyond and the figure of a woman in a long gown appeared and slowly walked towards me.

"This is my mother this time. How did I get her as my mother? Look at her hair!"

I looked back at my hand, "This is nothing like before."

My mother greeted me with a cheery, "Good morning," as she swooped me out of my bed, into her warm, chenille clad arms. I loved this familiar feeling of warmth and security, yet today was different as it came with a sense of arrival. Somehow this warm secure feeling alerted me to a new awareness. This new awareness was of a strong desire to feel and experience............what? I could not express it as thought, as expression and thought were yet to become completely connected in my new being. I only knew that it was a feeling of being everywhere and with everything, yet nothing. I knew that morning that this feeling was what I must discover, or perhaps re-discover, as I was certain that I had experienced it before. A long time ago - before any thoughts took shape; a long time ago, before my hand was formed.

My mother carried me down the hallway and turned into the lounge room, and then again into the kitchen. This had been the morning ritual, but this time it seemed to have more meaning because this time I had thoughts. I knew then that I must re-discover that experience that I could barely remember, yet absolutely yearned for.

That day had clarity like no other.

I had definitely landed in this time.

Thud.

I was placed in my high chair. As gently as my mother placed me there, it always felt like a thud. I looked in awe as she lowered my chair's tray and did up the lock. I studied my mother's face- such curly hair and clear, blue eyes. Her skin was so white. It almost seemed to glow. I watched my mother prepare porridge. I watched her every move with intensity and savoured this more than the porridge itself.

"Here we are," chirped my mother.

Initially, I was never a willing recipient of food.

"Come on! Here comes the plane!"

My mother's cheerful encouragement always met with an unresponsive stare.

"OK. First I will feed your star," my mother continued and zoomed the spoonful of nourishment toward the smiling star transfer on the back of my chair. I giggled and watched as my mother continued zooming until all my chair's transfers had been fed.

"It's your turn now. Here it comes!" She continued happily.

I could enjoy my food now; now that all my transfers had been fed, and now that I could think about it. Thoughts had allowed me to land completely and to remember that landing.

I loved just experiencing the days at my seaside home. My parents' company and walks in the stroller had been my favourite experiences until the day when my thoughts arrived. Once I could think, I became more aware of this new world of *this time*. In this new world of *this time* my legs were very different too. They were so different that people thought that being taken for walks in my stroller would be the closest that I would ever get to walking as this was one thing that my legs were definitely *not* designed to do. I would often stare at my legs as if I was searching for an answer or at least a clue as to why they were so different to everyone else's. I was aware of the endless hours that my mother would spend entertaining me by reading stories and playing games that she had devised in an effort to get her precious child to begin to walk.

When evenings grew near, my mother and I would wait for my father to get home from work. He was a plumbing teacher at the local college. This meant that he had school holidays to spend with his precious family. My father would pack the car and we would all head south down the highway to spend this holiday time divided equally between Sydney and Wollongong where my grandparents lived.

My dad was my hero. He was so strong and tall. I loved it when he carried me around as I felt as if I was almost seeing things from the top of the world. He understood me and he spent hours just playing with me. He accepted me just the way I was – crooked legs and all, but my mother was different. No matter what anyone said she always believed that I would walk. There was absolutely no way that she would ever accept the words *crippled* or *disabled* into my reality. She had even managed to find doctors who would allow her this dream and in the fifties, this was no easy feat.

As a result of mum's determination, a regular feature of our trips to Sydney would always be at least one long appointment with these well-meaning specialists. Each one searched in his own often painful way, to determine what went wrong and more importantly how to fix it. I could remember pain long before I could recall any thoughts. Pain seemed to precede my arrival here. Pain came in tumultuous waves as these specialists attempted to put my malformed legs into words. Words would put them into a category so that then they could attempt a remedy. The results of these assessments told them that there was no category and therefore no remedy. The only remedy was acceptance. My parents just had to accept that their child was crippled and intellectually disabled or retarded as people said back then.

Sometimes the memories of the pain leading up to this conclusion would overwhelm me, as I am sure the news of their conclusion overwhelmed my parents. Sometimes when a person wore white it would bring the memory of pain flooding back into my reality and I would scream until the poor unsuspecting person left. This flood would also come in the dark. My parents had set up a bed on the lounge where I would lay, my back to the T.V., examining my favourite objects until sleep would finally take over and often bring me peace. Sometimes I didn't examine anything. Instead I would experience that feeling of being everywhere and with everything, yet nothing. This was more than a feeling of peace.

Most nights I did not know that I was swimming in darkness. Other nights were not so kind, as they took me to places that I did not understand. These places were not "the stuff that dreams are made of." These were very different. In all these places I was able to walk.

One place was filled with terror as I was surrounded by boulders falling all around me. I ran and ran to escape them but every time I dreamt of this place one of the boulders would eventually fall on top of me. The feeling was excruciating, as the weight of the world came down on my shoulders and as hard as I struggled, it pinned me down with suffocating pressure. I would always wake up screaming.

Just as this place was filled with horror, another land that sleep took me to was exquisitely beautiful. Although, I didn't recognize the figures that dwelt there, in the dream they were so familiar to me. They too were of stone. This stone was beautifully sculptured into huge figures of a human. This human form was carved many times and in many positions. Some were standing, some were sitting cross-legged and my favourite one was reclining on his side with children crawling all over him. I loved this figure and I felt great peace and joy from walking around him in my dream. All these figures were outside and I always entered the grounds through a beautifully carved archway. I was so small in comparison to these sculptures of pure beauty. I always felt so serene. This feeling always stayed with me when I woke up from the dream of this place that was so unlike the other place of stone.

Sometimes I ran barefooted through a jungle to a village. I was always running from some kind of invisible threat. In my dreams I knew what it felt like to use my legs not just to walk but to flee. I could recall the experience and it was always clearly there within reach. I could even recall seeing my bare feet swooshing in and out of folds of beautiful but ragged cloth that I could feel clothing me. My recollections of the well-worn paths through the jungle were so vivid that I could taste it.

Although I always was running from something, I did not ever recall a feeling of fear there. I always stopped running when I would feel the jungle clear and I came to a particular place that I knew was my home. It was a strange dwelling with a thatched roof and walls made from some kind of woven plants .The walls only came half way up to the roofs. People always greeted me in a language that was foreign, yet I always understood it in the dream. For someone that could not take even take a step, it was amazing that in all my dreams, I could walk and even run for my life.

Another experience I can vividly remember in these early dreams was floating.

Again this was a clear experience. In this dream I was always floating above a sea of balloons or at least that is what it looked like. As I looked down at the balloons, one would always burst. This seemed to create a chain reaction and all the balloons would individually burst into flames, Sometimes, I would find myself on the ground during this reaction, experiencing pure horror without any visuals that I could recall. I could never understand this dream and I didn't like it at all. I would wake up screaming until my mother scooped me up into those warm safe arms and cradled me back to sleep in my parent's bed. I don't remember experiencing dreams of dolls or fairy story places, just these places, over and over again.

At the time I could not give them meaning even with thoughts. I decided that they had no meaning other than to let me feel what it was like to walk so that I could at least have an attempt at avoiding the box that so many doctors wanted to slot me into.

All these dreams began long before my memory of landing, as these dreams were experiences that I had. They were very different to thought.

After landing, I remember thinking some very important thoughts.

Thought was very different to a thing happening to you.

Thoughts were needed to carry these things that happen in your mind.

Experience seemed to just happen but thought came from your will.

Feelings could be experienced before thoughts ever came.

Sometimes I would play with this new ability to think. I often chose to turn this ability off and try to just exist the way I must have before I remembered landing in this very confusing world. Slowly the thought tap would be turned off and words that had been so important with thoughts attached to them became melodious sounds, or even just strange noises. This game would sometimes truly take me back to that time of pure existence that I somehow remembered and at times wouldn't have minded returning to.

Now that I had landed complete with thought, life became more complicated. I could no longer experience it as a never ending movie. Now I had to participate. That first thought that "this is my hand" carried with it the almighty awakening of my ego and with that came a hidden but overwhelming sense of responsibility to find that feeling of being everywhere and with everything, yet nothing. It also gave me an eerie sense that I didn't somehow belong to my dear family, but that somehow I had landed there by mistake.

Once I had landed here, in the realm of thought, this world became *my* world.

It made it more exciting but even more complicated. I began to learn the songs and games that my mother played. I could picture the world that words painted for me. Once I could recall thoughts, I could remember and make plans. My first plan was to walk.

"I have to!" I remember thinking, "Because I can't get the feeling of being a part of everything and being everywhere if I can't even get *anywhere*. I just have to walk!"

Chapter 2

The Lady on the Table

It was my second birthday. I enjoyed my presents. I loved to look at my beautiful birthday cards. My mother's voice sounded even more exquisite to me as my parent's sang "Happy Birthday." They must have felt proud now that they could safely reject the intellectually disabled label that doctors had attempted to attach to their little pride and joy. It was obvious to everyone that the doctors were wrong. My endless chatter was a testimony to this fact.

Was I a cripple? Well there seemed to be no doubt about that; at least, no doubt to everyone, except my parents. They had named me "Lisa" meaning "oath of God" or "consecrated by God", so surely the strength of my name coupled with their strong catholic faith would help to make a miracle happen-that, as well as all their hard work. They taught me to pray for miracles and help and they banished any obvious form of negativity towards me learning to walk, whether it was in the form of neighbours, well- meaning friends or doctors.

That birthday felt like a lifetime away from the time when they had feared defeat. This fear came after a stay at a hospital that was going to assess me in an attempt to give me a disability label. The stay itself was an experience that I simply recalled as pure pain. My parents agreed and could recall every detail. As soon as I arrived at this institution, I was stripped of not just my own clothes, but of every personal item that may have offered any comfort to me. I was left alone in that place. My parents were not allowed to visit me until the weekend. They had not even recognized me when they came to visit. Immediately my mother made arrangements for me to leave that place. She told the staff that I was "fretting away."

"No, no Mrs. Barron. You just have to accept that this is just how children like this, are.

She does not even know when you are gone."

This was the response that my mother's reactions caused and it was enough for mum to immediately stop listening to this set of doctors and to stubbornly take me home.

As soon as I returned home I began to thrive once more to the amazement of those doctors.

"Well, well Mrs Barron. You certainly are a lesson for us all. We'll have to re think our policy on parents' visits as it seems these children do fret after all."

This was the response that my mother tells me that her return with me caused. They then marvelled at how many other families would be spared the pain of separation, all because of one woman's stubborn decision.

As my parent's stood around the birthday girl that day, they no doubt looked back at all the small victories that they had won during their daughter's first years of her life. They would have been proud of their small family's achievements. No doubt, they prayed that night as they did every night, that their daughter would walk by her next birthday. Meanwhile, I was lying in bed, determinedly planning that one day soon I would walk. It had to be soon because I was so tired of always looking up at everything. There was not one thing that I could see other than the ground and whatever lay on it, without craning my neck to look up, or worse still without waiting for someone to pick me up. If I could feel myself walking in my dreams, then I must be able to do it in my real life. I would do it soon. I simply must, I thought.

My family was due to visit Sydney. I could tell that this visit would be special. I could feel it. I tingled with anticipation all the way to my grandparents' home. It was dark when we arrived. The house smelt beautiful as we entered it. It always had a special smell: one of a mixture of flowers, my grandfather's tobacco and my grandmother's perfume that never seemed to come from any bottled fragrance but rather it was her own sweet fragrance. I breathed in that precious scent.

I loved their house. I especially loved my grandmother's ornaments. There was one delicate ornament of a lady sitting with a beautiful hat on. She had long fingers poised in the most elegant way as if to allow a butterfly to land on her finger. This delicate beauty sat on a table but I didn't get to see it properly unless someone nursed me while standing up.

I remember lying in my father's arms as he carried me to bed that night. I nestled into the bed my grandparents had prepared for me and into the thoughts of seeing my precious Nar, in the morning. I had named my grandmother Nar and she was like an angel to me. I loved the way she sang every morning and whistled melodiously in answer to the birds outside. I loved the way that she disappeared into her room every morning to say her prayers. Nar always prayed to St Anthony and to Saint Francis that her beloved granddaughter would walk. She did this every morning and every evening. Nar taught me to pray too. She also taught me to believe that God would let me walk. She taught me to believe in and to pray for this miracle to happen. I loved the place that these prayers took me because it was a place of experience, not thought. It reminded me of the desire that I had to find that feeling or experience of being all and everywhere, yet nothing but here. I said those prayers that night as I lay in my cosy bed.

The morning sun shone brilliantly through my bedroom window the next day.

I could hear the birds heralding a new day. I longed to race out and join them but instead I had to lie in bed and wait for the first sound of footsteps down the hall, as that sound heralded the start to my new day. Every day I would call the first adult that could carry me out of my bed. I still had that special feeling from the night before. Tingles of anticipation came as I heard my father's footsteps.

"Daddy! Daddy!" I called.

"Good morning my Snorky and how are we this morning?" he called cheerfully, as he came into my room. "Here we are! Ready? Up we go," he continued, as he scooped me up into his arms.

He carried me into the dining room and sat me in a chair. I felt different. How or why I didn't even consider. I just knew that I felt different. In fact, the whole day felt different. My father came back with a bowl of porridge. I played another game that I enjoyed. I pretended that I couldn't think so that I could look around without thoughts- the way I saw things before I landed. When I did this, things around me had no meaning. They were simply different shapes of varying degrees of beauty that were like patterns on a canvas. There were no thoughts to confuse things. I played this game now because my thoughts about porridge were about to take away the very special feeling that I was sharing with this beautiful morning. I ate my porridge without any thoughts. I did not even bother to remember that I didn't like to eat. I just ate until the bowl was empty.

"Well done Snorky!" smiled my father, as he wiped my face and cleared my dish. He carried me into the lounge room and sat me on the floor, not far from the table where my precious lady sat.

"I'm not waiting for anyone to pick me up to see her," I vowed in one single burst of desire and tingles. "I'll walk there all by myself. I'll see her whenever I want to. I am going to walk." I uttered every word to myself and with every fibre of my being.

I focused on that table. I looked at it with all my attention. I pictured myself walking towards the table on my own. I pictured the delicate lady. I imagined seeing her from her own height for the first time. I replayed the experience of my dream walks. I knew that now was the time to do it, in this life.

No one was there- just me and this wonderful feeling that was slowly changing to determination to make my dreams of walking a reality. I stared ahead and then looked at the table. I looked down at my legs and I drew them up until my knees were under my chin. With all my strength I leant forward, using my hands to balance me, until for the first time my feet had all my weight on them without anyone holding me up. I don't remember how I got from that position to standing up with sight fixed firmly on that table but I did it. Then, I took my first teetering step towards my beloved lady.

I did not think. I just kept those legs moving, the way that I remembered from my dreams. The table grew closer and before I knew it, I had the smooth timber of that table flat against my palms, as I stood eye to eye with my beloved ornamental lady. That lady had an incredulous beauty now and the table she sat on, the tallest of my grandmother's nest of tables, had transformed itself into the most beautiful table that I had ever seen. I squealed with delight. The sound pierced my mind's silence and sounded like the sweetest note that I had ever heard.

It reached my parents and brought them running to the lounge room where they stood motionless at the door. It was as if they had never heard a squeal like that before. They had run expecting anything but this new sight that met their eyes. The silence of their stunned stares seemed to last forever, but it was just a moment frozen in time.

"My God" was all that my mother could utter.

"I left her in the middle of the floor," whispered my father. By now my grandparents had arrived to witness this unbelievable yet long awaited event.

"It's nothing short of a miracle ....I can't believe..." continued my mother.

I stood transfixed, no longer staring at my ornament but at the faces of my family. I still did not have a single thought but just a great feeling of joy. I put my head back and laughed. I laughed with all my heart. My family joined in and my father scooped me up in his arms, kissing my cheeks. Mum joined in the hug and it felt fantastic. I knew that I was the reason that everyone was happy, really happy. I remember thinking that this felt so good and it was so unexpected because all I was trying to do was see the ornament.

My father put me down on the floor and sat back down on the lounge. My mother and grandparents joined him. All eyes were on me. I looked at them with a smile and focused once more on my twisted legs. Without a thought I drew on that energy of desire one more time and slowly raised my legs up to repeat this process of walking. I teetered for a moment but kept walking towards my family for the first time in my life of almost three years. It felt incredible, much better than in my dreams.

My grandmother was the first to speak. "Do you know whose feast day it is? We've all prayed to him for help and to think it's happened on his day!"

It was St Anthony's feast day. He was known as the performer of miracles. Tears of joy welled in every adult eye.

It is a great event to walk in everyone's life, but to do it when your legs were badly deformed and you've been labelled a cripple in the experts' eyes was a huge event. My shins were severely bowed and I could twist them outwards and inwards without moving the rest of my legs. My feet had no arches so my ankle bone was on the ground. They were twisted inwards and had a big bone that stuck out of the side of them that should not have been there. I also had a huge gap between my big toes and the next ones. My legs were never meant for walking, but they were.

    My adventure was just beginning.

Chapter 3

Beyond the Horizon and the Other Side of Eyelids

I loved to walk. I walked or attempted to run everywhere. However the price of preserving this incredible experience involved many other experiences of a different kind. The trips to the specialists took on a whole new dimension. Now that I walked it was necessary to somehow ensure that I could continue to do so because Mother Nature had failed to give any such guarantees. Although my legs were miraculously supporting me as a three year old, they would not be able to do so once I was fully grown at around sixteen, because of their deformities. The only solution was to re-structure my legs.

Once again, this was not at all easy in 1960's. This would have been impossible if it was not for Doctor Gordon Colvin. He was a Macquarie Street specialist; one of the best in Sydney. He was my knight in shining armour. I had absolute trust in him and was a willing participant in every single plan that he, together with my parents, made to ensure that I would be a walking adult. I always understood though, that not even Dr Colvin could promise that anything would work for sure. I always thought that if I made it to my sixteenth birthday walking, then, I'd know that I was safe from becoming a cripple. It didn't worry me though because I had absolute faith in miracles now.

Dr Colvin seemed to order new tools of torture for me to wear each year to be sure that I walked safely and that my legs learnt to walk the right way. I never knew the feeling of walking with bare feet. Heavy callipers and ankle length boots were a part of my normal dress now. I had to wear them before my feet even touched the floor each morning, and they were only ever removed for a bath before bed time. Once I got used to the feel of them I loved my new style legs. They let me live my dream. They let me see the top of things, explore my world, and best of all to walk along holding hands with my mum and dad. I thrived in the freedom that walking gave. I could walk around the garden, play with the other kids in our street and make awesome cubby houses in the surrounding bush.

One day had that special feeling about it, like the day I walked, but nothing remarkable happened.

It wasn't the day I caught my fattest tadpole or my first frog, nor was it the day I discovered the fairy glen in the bush.

Instead it was a day spent alone in my own backyard. The sky was a brilliant blue and the sun seemed to have a special shine to it that day. It made me stop at the top of our steps and look out at the yard. I had my sick doll tucked under my arm and was going to go to collect weeds that I pretended were a special cure for her. White clover danced in a sea of green grass. It was a magical sight to my eyes. I looked out to the horizon and beyond. I focused my attention there somehow. When I focused on this "beyond", I could somehow feel how beautiful it was. I felt this without thought. I then somehow saw this "beyond." It was a beautiful scene that I did not understand. As I looked deeper into the scene I became elated because I began to recognize the people in the scene as my big family but my parents were not there. These people were all dressed in strange but very beautiful clothes. They looked as though they had all gathered for a special picnic. At least that's how it seemed to me as a three, going on four, year old. This experience probably only lasted a minute, but in that moment I experienced a glimpse of what would be the future. I felt so good.

It was a moment that seemed to be eternal and that is what it became. It was indelibly etched in my mind to be recalled as vividly as the memory of the birth of a first child. The moment passed and I went on to collect my weeds. I revelled in the fact that I had actually felt a little of *that* lost feeling that I was searching for. I felt like I had found some long lost family and I knew that I had found it somewhere out there- past where you can see and where you don't need to think.

I enjoyed many other moments like these, not all with a beautiful vision, but all had a certain feeling —a feeling that allowed me to have an incredible sense of true belonging -of being a part of everything and everyone, yet owned by no one, not anyone, and hampered by absolutely nothing.

Other times I battled with the weight of humanness that felt like it would suffocate me. This happened when I was faced with long, lonely stays in hospital, sleepless nights brought on by parents' bitter arguments, pain, or overwhelming childhood fear caused by all sorts of things including angry parents and children that liked to throw stones at me. I learnt that when these kinds of things happened I could not flee but I could certainly retreat. This place of retreat was deep within my existence. To reach it I would close my eyes and dive with my mind into the vast space of my being. It was like travelling in space, because although my eyelids were closed, I had some kind of vision "on the other side of my eyelids", as I used to try to explain it. This vision was breathtakingly beautiful. I didn't know what to call it.

I learnt to read a year before I started school. I remember first seeing pictures of my inner world in a children's encyclopaedia and being amazed to learn that it was called outer space. I remember thinking that this place shouldn't be called this because it was really the same as my inside space. I thought about this and decided that whenever I closed my eyes and went deep enough, I was exploring my own "outer space" that was somehow on the other side of my eyelids. It was all inside of me.

Some of the sights and experiences of my inner world were not to be found anywhere in my outside world. These were the experiences of the inner garden that I would see. This garden was made up of different levels that I could dive into. At each level, there was a different flower. My thoughts had chosen to use this word "flower" to name this inexplicable find because flowers were the only things that even came close to resembling this inner discovery. However, these flowers possessed extra qualities. They had no stem but instead they floated and spun in ponds of colours that changed according to the different levels that I managed to dive to.

Although I could choose to go to this inner garden, I had little control over the depths that I could reach at each visit. Sometimes I could not dive any further than the first pond. Other times I could easily manage to go quite deep. These flowers were always seen from an aerial view. At each level or depth the flower also changed, but the same flower was always found at the same depth. The beauty of these floating flowers always left me with the feeling I was looking for. I never took thoughts to my garden. I had no awareness of the outside world when I was there. I was just aware of being one with my garden and being free. I loved this inner sanctuary. The more I explored it the more I came to firmly believe that this world was definitely worth exploring as much as the outside world was. I didn't understand it and I certainly had no words to describe it other than those childhood favourites of "pretty" and "beautiful."

At first I only went there to escape from negative experiences, but that changed. As I got older I went there anytime whether to escape from boredom during long car trips through heavy traffic or dull lessons, as a way to get to sleep or just because I felt like it. This retreat was always with me. I never talked about these experiences. They had no thought attached to them when they happened so I couldn't really tell anyone about them. I just kept them.

Another more normal retreat perhaps was my belief in God. I was everyone's "miracle child," or at least to everyone in our parish. After all, I was a walking talking member of the community, and that was miracle enough for me to prove the existence of a higher power that knew more than even the doctors. I loved Mary, the Holy Mother too, as Nar always told me that if you prayed to her she would talk to her son, Jesus and things would work out for you. I wanted to be another St Bernadette or one of the children of Fatima and have direct contact with Mary. I thought that if I could just pray long and hard enough and of course look the part, it would certainly happen. I would dress up in one of my mother's skirts and drape a scarf over my head attempting to keep it there with bobby pins and then put a garland of clover flowers on the top, so that I looked just like St Bernadette. I don't know why I thought Bernadette wore a garland of clover flowers.

My favourite place to pray was in a grotto with my favourite statue of Mary made in the image that appeared when Bernadette saw her in Lourdes. There was a grotto like this in the grounds of a church in the next suburb that was fifteen minutes away by car. I would beg my parents to take me there on the weekends. Although they were practising Catholics, they were not overly devout and would have preferred to stay home and relax together on a Saturday afternoon but sometimes they would give in to my nagging and off we'd go. Sometimes I drove them crazy I'm sure, by insisting that I wore my Bernadette outfit all day. I only remember them giving in to that once.

Mary never answered my requests to talk to me, but I always imagined that she knew that I was there, and that left me with a whisper of that sought after feeling that was so hard to explain. This whisper of a feeling was like a fine thread that kept appearing just out of grasp but I loved it and I loved my inner retreats.

I had learnt from my family and church sermons that God was meant to come back one day. I decided that this was going to happen when I was alive. It even occurred to me at some point that He might have even wanted me to help Him to save the world because otherwise, why would He waste so much time on getting me to walk?

It was obvious that the world needed saving. I'd learnt from church that the world was filled with evil and that God was upset about this. I learnt that we had to love each other and it was very obvious to any disabled child that life is not like that. I learnt that we were meant to be one family, but I already knew about war through television and relatives' stories. I was taught that God only lets special people suffer - people like saints and martyrs and even Jesus. I knew I had lots of suffering because of my legs. That coupled with everyone calling me an angel and saying that my walking around was a miracle, convinced me that somehow I would help God to save the world. I was only four so who could blame me?

Since my landing I had learnt a lot about my inner worlds of dreams, nightmares, feelings, my inner universe and my inner garden. I'd also learnt to read a little bit and had learnt lots of games and things from my family. Despite all this learning I couldn't wait to start school. All the kids in the street had started school because they were older than me and I felt left out. I couldn't wait to start to write and to learn all about everything. I longed so desperately for this school experience that sometimes I would pack my little blue and white checked suitcase with my pyjamas and run away to the school nearby. I have no idea why I packed pyjamas for school.

Once, I even made it into a classroom. I sat up so proudly, absolutely certain that no one would think my presence unusual at all. I even felt confident that I would be able to repeat the procedure from that day on. I didn't even notice that I was the only one not dressed in maroon and gold or that I was the only person wearing callipers and boots. I felt certain that I fitted in perfectly. I sat like the perfect pupil as the teacher passed out craft scissors. I can still recall that moment when he reached my desk and handed me the shiniest pair of scissors in the world. They felt so cold and grown up when I held them. The moment was changed very quickly when I heard a familiar voice at the classroom window.

I remember the horror as I turned my head to the window to see my mother's face. It had an expression that I knew very well. It happened when poor mum had passed feeling just a little bit worried and gone to fear. The resulting expression was a glimpse of fear and then very quickly it changed to relief and then anger. It sounds like this should take a long time but let me tell you it happened in a blink. It was usually followed by a lot of angry, loud parent talk to impress on me that this was something never to be repeated. However I did just this. I repeated it a number of times because I felt that I had every right to be in that magical place called school.

My favourite game was to set up a classroom at home with teddy bears and dolls as pupils and myself as teacher. I had a blackboard complete with duster and chalk, but best of all I had a real brass school bell. My grandfather had found it and donated it to my little school. The sound of that bell was the best one in the world but I longed to hear it from further away as then it would mean that someone else was ringing the bell to call me to class. It would mean that I was a real pupil at a real school.

One day before I started school, I had to go for an eye test. Mine was not a routine check but rather a trip to a specialist who was going to do special tests to determine why it was that one of my eyes was not like everyone else's. Thankfully it had a normal shape, but exactly half of my left eye was brown while the other half was blue as was my right eye. Other specialists had decided that this was not genetically possible as both sets of my grandparents as well as my parents had blue eyes. They convinced my parents that this could be an ominous sign, and that they should have my eyes examined by a different specialist. As if they hadn't put enough fear into my poor parent's heads, not to mention my own, now they had added the possibility of blindness. The test results proved that this was not going to be the case, and that the brown was some kind of genetic mutation.

However, for me the results of the visit to this specialist were far from normal. At some time during the visit, I realised that I could see all the little bits of everything. I saw that everything was made up of little silvery bits moving very rapidly. On some surfaces of things, these tiny bits moved rapidly from both within and all around the surface, but on some surfaces, they moved rapidly but only on the spot. Where there were no silvery bits it was dark. Yet I could still see the colour of the surface. I had no idea what this meant other than it was very interesting and a little bit unnerving at first. However once I got used to it and was sure I was not going blind, I began to enjoy it.

I especially enjoyed looking at the white surgery wall for the rest of the visit. I enjoyed it not only because I was now no longer afraid of the colour, but because the wall was much more than a wall.

This wall had somehow shown me its own universe. This thought stayed with me as I watched all the silvery bits that made up the universe of every object in the room.

"Everything has its own universes too and I can see them!" was the exciting thought that jumped into my mind when I left the specialists. My thought was completely different to my mother's as hers was just one of relief that my vision was normal.

So the first five years of my life were nothing at all normal, whatever that word means. However, I had no concept of this because my world was filled only with people who were very kind. My mother ensured that none of them would ever make me aware that I was different.

The first time that I remember feeling that I was different to other people, was when I was watching my beautiful older cousin, Kerry dance in ballroom competitions. She was never aware of it but she was the first person to make me very aware that I was different. Kerry danced with her partner in beautiful ball gowns, whilst I sat and watched in my boots and callipers. I felt a sadness that made me want to be like Kerry, so much - to be able to dance and wear such beautiful shoes as well as the dresses. This was the first time that I experienced what I later learnt was jealousy. Once I even cried when my grandmother gave me a beautiful fake fur shawl, just like Kerry's so that I would not feel left out. Kerry left to go to her dancing competition while I sat under the Christmas tree wearing my pyjamas and the shawl. I felt as though that shawl mocked me as it draped elegantly around my shoulders. Perhaps what made things harder was the heavy awareness I now had.

I was not at all like other people.

Another experience that showed me very really that it was sometimes hard to feel a part of everything, was the arrival of my younger sister just before I started school.

I had always wanted a sister; I can remember begging my mother to get a baby. I had seen how easy it was when we had visited my mother's friend in hospital and saw her new baby. We had stood in front of a glass window where there were lots of babies on the other side. People came up to the window put some money in the donations box and then the nurse showed them the baby that, to my childish mind, they had bought. I watched people put in threepence and they even got to have a baby. I begged my mother when I got home to simply put threepence in the box so that we could buy a baby. I knew that my poor mother had a lot of threepences because she collected coins. As it turned out the box was to collect donations for a charity.

Finally my mother fell pregnant. The reality of my mother having a baby was something that I literally could never imagine. I knew that her stomach was very big and I suggested one day not long before the birth of my sister, that mum should put a pin in her stomach so that the balloon that she was hiding under her dress would go down. When poor mum stopped laughing, she told me that it wouldn't work.

Soon after that day, my world burst when we went to Sydney and to my horror my parents left me with my grandparents, while my father took my mother to hospital to have my long awaited sister.

I had no understanding that this sudden separation from my mother had anything to do with getting a baby sister. After all I had seen for myself how simple it was. All I knew was that I was away from my mother. I was just petrified. This was separation and that usually meant pain. I suddenly saw my beloved grandparents as the future instigators of this pain and for the first time I remember fighting. I fought with them to let me be with my mother and accused them of lying when they tried to tell me that she would be back with a new baby brother or sister. How my beloved grandparents ever dealt with this time I will never know, but they did and so did I.

After the longest days of my short life, my mother walked through the door with a little bundle that I absolutely adored. This was my own baby sister called Madeline. I started school soon after we came home. I began to learn that I was very separate from my family when I went to school and that unfortunately teachers were not always kind. As much as I loved school, there were days when I just wanted to stay at home with my mother. I began to feel a hot prickly feeling that was growing inside of me - one that made me want to be mean to my little sister . One that made me feel so mean.

When Madeline began to walk with ease I wanted to trip her over, so that she would get hurt and feel the pain that I felt watching her walk so easily. I don't remember actually tripping her over, but I'm sure I must have at some time. What confused me was that whenever Madeline did hurt herself I couldn't bear it. I felt as if it was my fault and I would give her big hug to try to make her smile again. I was so proud of my little sister but not so proud of myself.

When my sister, unlike me had no battle to walk, run or to do anything for that matter, I knew that I was even different to the rest of my family. Those thoughts of being in the wrong family returned. After all, when I landed I knew that my mother and my hand looked very different to what I had known. Whatever this all meant I certainly didn't know at just six years of age.

I just knew that it made me want to explore my inner world even more as now I had more situations that I felt a need to escape from. They were the times that made me painfully aware that I was not the same as most of the people around me. Whenever this happened and I retreated, I would forget thoughts and just feel that wonderful freedom of being everywhere and nothing, yet a part of everything.

Doctor Colvin always reassured me. This was another reason that he was my hero. He always promised that I would wear normal school shoes when I started school and party shoes before I was a teenager. I believed completely in him, and bit by bit he fulfilled these promises.

First he allowed me to shed my callipers and boots for school shoes. Next he let me shed my shoes for white sandshoes, in time to march like everyone else at the beginning of the school's athletics carnival. I loved that carnival even though I knew that I was guaranteed last place in every race. I had somehow decided that to come last was just as important as first place, because without last place, coming first had no meaning and if suddenly we were all told to turn around in the race, I would be first! When I came last in every race at school, I always remembered this and I never felt sad. After all I was lucky to walk never mind run in a race.

The biggest hurdles were not at any sports events, but the ones that my hero put in front of me. There were only two of them, but it took monumental efforts to clear them. They were the operations to guarantee my walking ability.

Chapter 4

Plaster Prisons and Inner Retreats

My first clear memory of sheer and terrifying physical pain that had horrific thoughts attached to it was when I opened my eyes after my first operation just days before my eighth birthday. My shins had both been straightened. First, Dr Colvin had cut them in four places, and then he held them in place by using a metal bar through which he put four screws that were drilled straight through my shin bone. I was told they were pins and that there would only be three in each leg. The pain was unbearable and I was kept on a cocktail of drugs for days after this ordeal.

Well-meaning relatives came bearing gifts of every fashionable doll - Barbies, Cindy, and Princess Pattie - complete with boxes of beautiful clothes to dress them in. This was any other child of the sixties idea of heaven, but not mine. I screamed how much I didn't want their presents and would not even speak to them, much to their horror. Their saintly Lisa acted like a demon. I wanted nothing but the pain to go away because until it did, nothing else existed. I knew that all the pretty things in the world would not get rid of it for me.

This was my first and most powerful lesson on the futility of possessions, as compared to a driving inner force. Again and again I would turn my back on this materialism, and dive into my inner universe instead. It was only here that I could escape a painful reality, or as it was the reality of pain.

I also used my other tricks. I would pretend that I couldn't think and that words were just those melodious sounds with no meaning. When I did this, I caught a glimpse of that place where I was a part of nothing yet somehow everything. No matter how hard I tried though, I could not maintain this experience.

After this operation I was confined to a wheelchair for months. That's when I learnt that books were not just a way of learning but also a fantastic escape. I couldn't explore my real world by running around so instead I explored many worlds through books. I set off on endless adventures created by Enid Blyton, Louisa May Alcott, Robert Louis Stevenson and a host of other brilliant authors for a child of my times.

I couldn't do sport so I exercised the muscle of my brain. I kept up with my schoolwork at home. My friends would write out the daily timetable and collected my worksheets, so that I could fastidiously complete them the following day at home. When I came back to school not long before the yearly exams, and topped the class, the nun's felt even more assured that I was a miracle child.

When I reached Year Five and it was time to leave school once more to have the second operation, the nun's told me that my leg problem and all the associated pain was really a special blessing. It was my own cross to bear, just like Jesus had his to bear. They explained that this meant that I was closer to God than lots of other people. When they had finished this rather grotesque explanation of my special blessing, they nearly scared me to death by giving me a glow-in-the-dark crucifix, to hold on to when the pain got too hard to bear.

All I could think of as I held the crucifix in my hand was, "They are comparing my next operation to the pain He felt on the cross. The last one hurt enough!"

Sometimes I feared that the only feeling that I would experience when I fulfilled the desire to feel a part of all yet nothing would be pain. Then, I felt a little bit embarrassed to think that they thought of me the way that they did.

The second operation proved not to be as painful as the first. This time I had an idea of what was ahead. In this operation, Dr Colvin removed the bones that jutted out on the inside of my feet and then took bones out of the lower part of my shin, and used them to build my feet up to have arches. This was a bonus because the plaster only imprisoned my legs to just below the knee so that I could bend my legs and so learning to walk again would not take so long.

This time I managed to smile and thank relatives who came bearing gifts.

No matter how much pain it caused, I got my toes to move after the operation, as I knew that this would get me home faster.

This time I was an old hand at the wheelchair so I was somehow spared the sore muscles.

This time around I even managed to learn some yoga exercises so that I could keep a little bit of tone in my muscles and so I prevented them from looking like the limp rubber bands that they were last time they shed their plaster prison. Another bonus was that this plaster prison was to last three months instead of six, so learning to walk was easier the third time around.

Once again I kept on top of my schoolwork by scheduling my days as they had been the day before at my school.

Once again I returned to school after conquering the obstacle involved in learning to walk in yet another different pair of legs. This was to be the final model.

Once again I topped my year when I returned after another long absence. As a matter of fact I continued to top my year until my last two years at school.

I was the school's, my family's and my friends' pride and joy, and that, to me was an important thing. I had made people around me happy. I hadn't meant to do so well at school. It just happened because I couldn't explore the world the way other kids did. I had to do it through abstract forms which made me good at schoolwork.

I left primary school, dux of my school, a miracle child and best of all with a lot of friends. I had achieved what was meant to be the impossible. There definitely had to be a greater driving force for this to happen because a kid couldn't do that on her own. It was simple. There really had to be a god. I had learnt about God at home, at school and at church and I knew that God was meant to come again. I didn't just believe this but I actually somehow knew it, in every cell of my body. Every mini universe of my being knew that this would happen in my lifetime.

That desire to find that ancient feeling of being a part of everywhere and with everything, yet nothing was stronger than ever. Now I had learned more of my retreats, I knew I had experienced it, briefly, this time.

Chapter 5

Lisa and That Little Word I

High school brought with it a whole new set of challenges. My father had been promoted to head plumbing teacher at Randwick Technical College and my family was trying to sell up and move to Sydney. We were all looking forward to this idea but selling proved difficult. This meant my poor father would spend five days a week working in Sydney, away from his seaside home, and I missed him desperately. It also meant that I had to start high school at the local catholic girls' school. I had to move from my comfort zone where everyone knew of my battle to stand on my own two feet, into that vast new land of adolescence that we all must conquer, and once done like any conquered land it then shapes the very conqueror in such a subtle way that we are unaware of it. I found this new land to be very lonely. It forced me to begin to again think of how I fitted into the outside world. I began to realize that I was not a part of everything and everywhere but instead I began to feel lucky when I felt a part of anything at all.

I found out just how small and insignificant humanity was when I learned about how the earth's crust had a life force all of its own. Learning about dormant volcanoes and fault lines taught me this insignificance. Dormant volcanoes meant that anywhere where there was igneous rock, there was the possibility although extreme that it could suddenly come to life. This could even happen in my home town or worse still there was the very slim likelihood that the earth could open up in an earthquake. The knowledge of tsunamis also introduced another fear. What if there was an earthquake in another country and it created a wave big enough to swallow my seaside home?

For weeks after I learnt such knowledge I would lay awake imagining that at any moment we would be swallowed up in an earthquake. My poor parents had long since grown tired of my nightmares and sobbing cries. Now that I was older I knew that I had to cope with crippling fears from a rampant imagination that brought on the real and terrifying experience of panic. Thought and experiences were no longer the two separate things they had been when I was little. Once again, I escaped by diving into the sanctuary of my inner universe.

During the week, I had to deal with the fear of being laughed at in sport and P.E. lessons. I avoided this happening by hiding at the back of my classroom at the beginning of lunchtime. I'd stay in hiding until the end of sport when I'd sneak into the hat room and join my class to collect our belongings to leave for the day. Sometimes my parents did agree to write notes to excuse me from sports and PE lessons but should a nun feel particularly masochistic, not even a note could save me. Sometimes, this resulted in not just emotional injury as everyone laughed, but also physical pain as the exercise caused my bones to grind against those plates and screws.

I learnt to have a great fear of the nuns that taught me. In primary school I could avoid harsh corporal punishment simply by being a perfect pupil but these nuns dished out punishments that were degrading, cruel and unpredictable. I was petrified of my English teacher who threw my friend's desk through a partition and then knocked my friend backwards off her chair and through the same partition into the classroom next door. As a result of witnessing that I was frightened out of my wits into being a perfect pupil whose lowest mark on leaving this school was ninety percent.

No matter how hard I tried sometimes these punishments could not be avoided. I was regularly punished for dyeing the front of my hair because it was naturally lighter that the rest. This meant either a caning for lying, picking up rubbish or detention. Sometimes a nun would decide that my uniform was too short even though it was the required length of a couple of centimetres above my knee. She would rip down my wide hem in front of the entire school assembly and make me stand there until the end of assembly when she would take me to the principal's office where I would be caned. As if that wasn't enough I had to wear my box pleated uniform with the belt under my armpits, and the hem in tatters almost down to my ankles, for the entire day. I suffered ridicule from my peers and stern stares from all my teachers. I felt so hurt and humiliated. I began to wonder how these people who were supposed to be married to God could possibly be so mean. I knew that He wouldn't possibly approve of what they did.

I found it hard to form my identity. I began to think about that little word "I". I wondered how one single letter, one sound, had become the most unfathomable word there is in our language. Once I entered high school this word seemed to become even more important, especially to other people who seemed to insist that everyone learn all about their world of "I".

At high school I made a few new friends, but clung dearly to my old ones. They knew all of my weaknesses and battles. I needed them to shield me from strangers and to help me to put one foot in front of another along this very uncertain path of high school. The two that I clung to were Claire and Elizabeth.

Claire had been with me forever. Claire's mother had taken her to visit me before I had even started school. I loved Claire. When I was unable to go to school, Claire was the dear friend that always copied out the timetables and lessons each day for me to follow. Claire had been my lifeline to school.

I saw Elizabeth as some kind of saviour as the first time that I met her I was howling because I had just slammed my finger in the toilet door, sometime during my first week of kindergarten. I had felt so alone and once again pain had become everything in my immediate world, until Elizabeth appeared like an angel from nowhere. She comforted me and a strong bond was instantly formed. I still remember how ecstatic I felt when Elizabeth invited me to her birthday party. I gave her a beautiful white crocheted handbag and a white comb encased in a decorated silver cover. It felt so good to see Elizabeth's face when she saw this gift. She was a dreamer just like me. She loved reading too. So we shared endless adventures through our books. Elizabeth flattered me in a very different way. She was the first person to compliment me on my physical appearance. She told me that she thought I had pretty hair and nice hands. This was quite a novelty to me as most people couldn't see past the strange legs. These two friends were my protectors as I walked with great trepidation into this unknown world.

This high school journey definitely took me away from my inner world that I had enjoyed for probably way too long. I suddenly had to focus very much on the world around me in every possible way. I became very aware of my name Lisa. This Lisa was different to what I had been before my lessons in high school. This "Lisa" did not easily fit in. My name even sounded different when it was spoken by people here.

Lisa was very different.

Lisa was a goody-goody.

Lisa couldn't do sport or PE.

Lisa couldn't even run.

Lisa was someone that was often frightened of her peers and teachers who seemed so threatening that she couldn't bear to fail, yet success brought with it a different fear. This fear was one of ridicule. I learnt that continually coming top of my class was not something that brought popularity in this new school of life. I became painfully aware of my name. Sometimes I'd overhear people saying even worse things about me. In high school Lisa was not someone special but someone to make fun of or just despise.

At high school I learnt that it was not possible to feel a part of everything.

Chapter 6

Maths and Idealism

Not all was doom and gloom. Science lessons absolutely thrilled me, as I learnt more of the miracles of the universe. I marvelled at how everything was made of atoms. This explained why everything before my eyes was seen as small moving dots. I had given up asking family and friends about this phenomenon as their reaction quickly showed me that this was yet another way in which I was different. At least I could choose to not let anyone else be aware of this difference. As my teachers unfolded the microscopic beauties of chemistry and of the structure of molecules and atoms before me, I revelled at how each atom resembled a miniature universe.

Learning more about the solar system was both inspiring and awesome to me. Its vastness and the concept of no gravity, no sound; nothing; daunted me. Whenever I cast my thoughts to this marvel of creation I would experience a deep feeling that immediately recognized it as the place that I retreated to within. This somehow proved to me that we really did have a vast universe on the other side of our eyelids that was equally worth exploring as the one in space. It wasn't just a childish fantasy.

I also felt that before I landed, I must have existed in this universe as the more I acquired knowledge of it the more it rang ancient familiar bells and their sound gave me a deep sense of peace and comfort.

Maths fascinated me. I loved the mental gymnastics that it forced my brain into. I loved to prove things both in algebra and chemistry. My heart would thump with excitement as each mathematical problem fell into place on my page. I loved it when I could show my teachers short cuts to proving geometry problems by using a variety of theorems. These short cuts would either bring a stunned silence, a smile or a reddened face from my teachers, as they would turn to erase two chalkboards filled with the long winded proof that they had just demonstrated to the class.

When this happened my heart would thump even more wildly with excitement from the moment I raised my hand to make my contribution. I used to think that this was how it must feel to win a race or any other athletic event.

I also loved the fact that absolutely everything could be expressed as a mathematical function. Since this was true it then had to mean that even complete chaos or nothingness, still had a secret form of organization. This, I concluded was yet more proof of a God as only a highly superior intelligence could have organized creation in such an incredible way.

I left my first high school as dux of my school, but I didn't leave this school with many friends or as a miracle child.

Leaving that school felt like finally escaping a prison. The summer holidays unfolded, as did my parents plan to stay in this seaside home. Dad had been transferred back to Newcastle as head teacher. This was good news, as it meant we would be together again every day.

When we returned from visiting grandparents, I found that Rose and Claire had met and begun to hang around with a group of boys from different private schools that surfed at our beach. When I met these boys, I couldn't believe that some of them had been my friends in primary school. Those gangly boys had changed into handsome surfers.

Mum and Dad were happy to welcome this new circle of friends into our home because all of them were smart and would probably "go somewhere." Dad even let the boys leave their surfboards and wetsuits in our downstairs room so that they didn't have to carry them on the bus. This room became our hangout and music blared every weekend. We stopped going away every holiday as I no longer needed the specialists and Dad wanted us to enjoy our holidays at home.

Suddenly, I belonged to a cool group of friends. I loved them all because we all enjoyed philosophising about the existence of God, Nostradamus' prophecies of doom and gloom, global problems of all descriptions, and any other deep subject that captured our imagination. I loved to have my girlfriends sleep over, as I'd keep them awake all night telling them all my views of the world and how I felt sure that it was up to our generation to overcome all racism and materialism, and turn the world back to being a global family based on spirituality. I believed that man's biggest mistake was to invent the wheel. I believed this because I figured that if we had tried to use the power of our mind to shift things, instead of finding something to do it for us, then we would know how to use the other two thirds of our brain that no one seemed to know anything about. I even dared to confide in them that somehow God would come back, and we would get to meet Him or Her in our lifetime. I trusted them enough to tell them that people were crazy to pray and say that they believed in God, if they didn't ever think that miracles could actually happen, or that prophecies would not happen in their lifetime.

I knew about the reality of miracles, as the fact that I walked every day with a group of normal cool friends was a miracle in my reality. Doctor's even confirmed that it was a remarkable feat. My friends were very special people to be able to tolerate such heavy egocentric conversations, instead of usual teenage gossip.

Some nights seemed to take on a special energy, as if the power of our naïve yet wise words that shaped the stories of our futures as social and political reformists, beckoned a spiritual energy that looked on and made us tingle with the realisation that we were touching the real purpose of our lives and that it would all be a wonderful reality. I thrived on all these discussions, and naively believed that my friends would remain as dedicated to this cause as I was. Our long heavenly summer came to an end.

Don't get me wrong we were also normal teenagers in that we had our crushes on local surfers; we loved to listen to loud music and go to all the cool places. We even got slightly drunk and smoked marijuana sometimes. You can read libraries of stories about teenage drama, so I'm leaving it out because this other thread to our lives, is not often, if ever written about, and the time has come when it must be.

This thread in everyone's lives is so fine that it gets broken or forgotten somewhere yet it has so much to give to the chaotic patterns of life.

Chapter 7

Silver Commas, a Cross and Dreams

It was time to start our final years of schooling. This meant changing schools. Claire, Rose, our new friend from junior high school and I had bravely ventured from our small girls catholic high school, to the large co-ed local public school. This was even tougher than before, as this school had four times as many teenagers attending. I managed to relax in the classroom and once again relish every newly presented fact.

In senior high school I studied biology. I remember our teacher relating the physics principal that matter is neither created nor destroyed but simply transformed from one form to another. If this was true then that meant that a carbon atom in us could have been a part of the very first life on the planet. My brain raced on. If this was true then that meant that there must be eternal life because the energy that made up our soul or spirit didn't seem to transform into anything or at least my teacher didn't mention it, so, how could this energy be destroyed? It must just go on and on.

Chemistry classes fascinated me but also threatened me, as there were only three girls, including me in the entire class. The three of us stuck together. Our male chemistry teacher would often begin a lesson by statements such as, 'Well boys let's see what the damage bill caused by the girls will be like this lesson."

Everyone except Claire, our new very clumsy friend Ruth, and me would roar with laughter. Needless to say at times we would fulfil his expectations, with regards the breakages. Other times we would leave them stunned with our efficiency, speed and correct results. However the daily jokes coupled with some cruel comments tore at me. For the first time I began to feel as though I was struggling at school.

These senior years were very different ones. At first lunchtimes were spent avoiding girls who wanted to spit at me and call me "slut." I had first learnt the meaning of this word when boys older than me, who I so naively admired, yelled this out to Rose and I as we walked to the corner milk bar or to the beach. Rose had become a close friend.

"Virgin Mary" and "Lesso Lisa" were other names that we were called. These names were how I learnt about virginity and homosexuality for the first time, when I dared to ask the meaning of these awful sounding names. I heard these names so many times as I walked around my seaside village that was supposed to be home.

The more that I became aware of what Lisa was about in this lifetime, the less this place felt like home. How on earth had I come to be a part of a community that I could only ever observe and never be a part of, despite how hard I tried to fit in. At least that was how I felt until the school holidays came and I could just hang out with my cool group of friends. Our group slowly grew to include friends from our new school, who also shared our anti materialistic views.

Friday and Saturday nights were spent listening to Dylan, Neil Young, Donovan, Leonard Cohen, Jimi Hendrix, Janis Joplin, Led Zeppelin and anyone else that had a note of revolution to their music. We banned commercial musicians who stunk to us of mindless consumerism. Some of our friends even formed a band and wrote their own music. Some nights were spent listening to them practice while some of our group chose to fall in love, and experience the passion of a first kiss.

Whatever happened though, the highlight for me was always our discussions on the state of our planet and how we would transform it. One night stands out like no other in this time. It was one of those nights that seemed to have a special feeling about it. I did not recognize it as *that* ancient feeling of being a part of everything. I don't know if I would have recognized it even if it was, as it had been so long since I had delved into any of my inner retreats as my teenage ego was definitely well formed and thoughts were now my only inner experience.

I had become cynical about my church. I began to see its hypocrisy. For my entire school life I had watched nuns cane, belittle, beat and throw their young pupils. As I became a young adult I realised that the sermons that I had hungered for now nauseated me as more and more time was spent on money matters. The priest's favourite topic seemed to be to berate the parishioners because they were not donating enough money for church repairs and that as a result tiles were falling off the roof and could not be replaced, nor could leaking windows be repaired. I didn't know what sickened me the most; the fact that the priest was so materialistic as to waste time meant for saving souls on trying to increase saving of a different nature; or the fact that the people who sat there in their best Sunday fashions were too mean to give up their fashions for the sake of a church so that people like me could hear more from God and less from the parish funds.

Rose had decided that she was an atheist because of it. She visited her atheist boyfriend instead of attending church on Sundays. This worried me because to reject God completely meant to me a life of despair and an eternity in hell according to the church that I was still an obedient member of at this time.

Rose was staying at my house and we had exhausted the music selections and consumed enough cigarettes. We were lying side by side in the dark on the old divan downstairs pondering the meaning of life and stating possible reasons for life as it was now. It was summer. The bedclothes were folded at the bottom of our bed because it was way too hot to use them.

Suddenly I stopped talking and Rose gasped. There above us appeared the most beautiful light. It hovered above us in the shape of a cross that was similar in dimensions to the one that Christ was crucified on. It seemed to emanate a beautiful feeling. It was the same ancient feeling that I sought after and had almost forgotten. It stayed straight up above us and it filled my being with an absolutely divine experience.

Slowly Rose spoke in a whisper, "You see it too don't you?"

"Yes," I replied in an equally awestruck whisper.

"Tell me what you see," whispered Rose.

"No. You say it and then I'll know that it is real." I replied quickly considering Rose's new stance on God.

"It's a cross, like a crucifix. You know. You can see it too."

The image slowly broke up and small bright silver commas filled the darkness without lighting it up. When this happened, a cool breeze was felt for just a moment but the drop in temperature was enough to make both of us grab not just the sheet but the heavy homemade quilt as well. We shivered and hugged each other too overwhelmed for thought yet alone speech, until a wondrous sleep overcame us.

The next morning I couldn't wait to talk about this miracle of a different nature with Rose as I felt that somehow we had an encounter with God himself. That ancient feeling had been stirred deeply within me causing me to somehow feel almost transformed by this experience. I had so much joy in my heart when I asked Rose what she felt about what had happened. To my disbelief and complete incomprehension, Rose replied strongly and coldly, "I don't want to talk about it."

I was stunned and a little hurt by Rose's rejection. However the strength of it also excited me because it was proof that the night before was a very strong reality. It had to be as it obviously threatened Rose's new faith in atheism. What better proof could I have that this event was a vision of some kind, and not a case of wishful thinking. I remembered my childhood desire to search for that feeling. I definitely had felt it that night and somehow it was definitely associated with God or something divine. I decided then, that I did not believe in "the church", but I definitely knew that God and Jesus and all the rest were a reality, and not a belief.

This was the first of many spiritual events that I experienced during my senior high school years. These experiences managed to somehow reach into the future.

Once again, sleep became an unnerving realm as that was when these experiences of the future came.

When they occurred I would wake up in the morning with a different kind of "special feeling."

I felt it as soon as I opened my eyes. As the feeling filled my conscious mind it somehow searched for the reason for it. A dream from the night before would always come flooding back. As soon as this happened I would get a gut feeling that what I dreamt would actually occur. This would all happen in a matter of seconds.

The first time this happened, I had dreamt about a new primary school friend's home, in a neighbouring suburb. I had never been there to visit. I was invisible in the dream and I explored every nook and cranny. I opened cupboards, taking note of where the glasses, sugar, plates, cereal etc. were kept. Sure enough I was invited to her home and given permission to go the very next day. When I went to my friend's home, it was just as I had dreamt it. I surprised or shocked my friend by offering to get the glasses for afternoon tea and getting them without asking for any directions in a kitchen with numerous cupboards in which they may have been stored. I also managed a trip to the bathroom without any directions from my hostess. When my friend realized my uncanny knowledge, she giggled nervously and mentioned that my home must be set out the same. Even though I knew that this was not the case, I decided to accept that as an explanation. I don't remember any more of these dreams occurring until these turbulent final high school years.

The next one that I remember frightened me as it involved something far removed from inside knowledge of a friend's house. It forced me to take note whenever this feeling occurred in the future.

I woke up with a strong sense of that feeling. As I let my thoughts awaken me more, I remembered my bizarre dream. It had begun with me walking through an unfamiliar school playground at night in my school uniform to meet Rose and Claire at the bubblers. The dream then went to Rose's mother crying, as Rose began to tell us that her uncle had died. Rose's words then stopped and I was looking at another very unfamiliar scene, in which a man wearing a hard hat was knocked down by what looked like a small run away railway carriage. He was killed. This shocking scene was followed by a coffin slowly disappearing behind a curtain. The dream ended in black smoke with me standing back in the playground. I could not shake the unpleasant feeling of the dream and it was the first time that I had experienced this.

I chose to relate the bizarre events of the dream to Claire on our way to school because the unpleasant feeling had not completely gone. She assured me that there would be no way on earth that we would be at a school at night and so it couldn't come true. She also told me not to tell Rose, as Rose was still a sensitive budding atheist and this could really scare her and turn her against everything including us. I decided that Claire was right and eventually the feeling left with the memory of the dream.

I didn't remember the dream when our English teacher informed us that we were to attend a school debating competition that would be held at night in a school on the other side of Newcastle. I didn't even remember it when our teacher told us that we were all to attend wearing our full school uniform. The night of the debate arrived. I dressed in school uniform and left with my father.

When I arrived I saw Claire and Rose standing by the school's bubblers, talking. Rose seemed upset. When I asked what was wrong, I could not believe the reply. Her uncle had been killed in a freak accident at the steelworks. He was her mother's brother. He had been crossing the tracks when a runaway carriage hit him killing him outright. He was to be cremated in a couple of days. Claire just stood staring at me. I could feel my face drain of colour as memories of my dream, flooded my mind.

It was time for the debate. As we walked to the classroom, Claire said quietly to me

"I'd never have believed you if you'd told me after the accident, but I remember your dream and it's happened. God, how do you feel?"

I couldn't reply and I was spared, as Rose turned to wait for us. As a matter of fact we never spoke of it again. I had a lot of dreams like these. They always involved people dying and I would always wake up with a feeling that I learnt was called dread.

All of my dreams did share one common thread. They were all real experiences of a different dimension. No matter what they were about they all reminded me of that feeling that my very existence had craved for.

Chapter 8

The Lady on TV

Something that happened during my conscious hours should have scared me witless, but instead, I was excited because it revealed knowledge that I had craved for. I just wanted to tell all my friends about it. I felt sorry that they had missed out. It happened one night after my friends had been over for our usual evening of music and idealism. They didn't stay. It never occurred to me that maybe they were getting sick of my drawn out, predictable conversations.

I was unusually restless that night. No matter what I did, I could not sleep. I felt driven to go out to the lounge room and put on the television. My parents and sister were sleeping soundly as I crept out and turned the dial of the TV to see if I could find anything to watch. I didn't even realize that at two o'clock in the morning, there would be no television broadcasts. Late night television didn't exist yet. I didn't even bother to think that it was completely out of character to want to put television on at all, as I saw it as the supreme communicator of materialism.

I did find a program to watch. It was the broadcast of a beautiful woman giving a talk. She sat alone behind a white news desk. She had gleaming black hair with eyes equally as dark yet shining with light. She wore unusual white clothing and matching blouse. My world was so insular that I did not even know that this clothing was called a sari. I stood transfixed first by her sight and then by her words. She was talking about the problems of our planet.

I walked backwards to a chair and sat down, hardly believing what I was hearing. Her words were like water on a desert to me. They nurtured my very heart as she went on to explain that she had a plan that would transform our society. She explained that we were the source of our problems, as we had become too greedy for things. She followed by explaining that since we were the source, we could be the solution and turn it all around. She said that she was going to help us to do this by showing us how to get in touch with our true selves. I soaked these words up yet hardly believing what I was hearing. These were almost my words. This made this woman even more incredible to me. She ended by saying that we were not to worry about a thing because she would show us how to save the world and it would be simple.

When the lady had finished talking the T.V. broadcast suddenly became loud static and that was the end of all viewing. I quickly raced to turn the T.V. off as I was worried that the static would wake my family. Once again I felt a whisper of that feeling but this time it stirred something very deep inside of me with a subtle strength. It was like it was at the core of my inner universe and it took me to that core. It was that feeling of being a part of everything yet nothing and everywhere. I walked thoughtlessly to my room feeling totally at peace and then enjoyed a deep sleep.

The next morning I opened my eyes and *that* wonderful feeling came flooding back into my being along with the memory of that incredible television program. I eagerly got up and waited for the first of my friends to arrive after their surf. Dale, who was the older of my two friends that I had adopted as brothers, was the first person that I saw that morning other than my family, so I excitedly related the fantastic program to him. I told Dale that we would have to make sure that we watched it every week, as I was sure that it would be a weekly program because the lady had given the impression that she would be teaching different techniques to use to save the world.

Dale listened intently and then asked me at what time and on what station was this program. I knew that it was two o'clock in the morning by my parents lounge room clock but I did not have a clue as to what the station had been. That was the end of our conversation. Later that night Dale came over to visit. He asked me again about the program and what it had been about. I answered his every question in detail. At the end of my last answer, he sat back in the arm chair staring at me intensely. This was unnerving and even more so when he finally spoke to me.

"Lisa, I checked the T.V guide. I looked at every station's program in the TV guide, even the one in the daily paper and I don't know what you tuned into but it sure wasn't being broadcast by any

T.V station in this country. I've checked. There are no broadcasts that late ever - and certainly not any last night."

I didn't know what to say. I felt excited that I'd had some sort of special communication with someone that had stirred that feeling. I also felt disappointed as this also meant that none of my friends would have or could in the future, ever tune in to this beautiful lady's enlightening talks. It also meant that I would not be able to talk about this subject again, because to do so would make me different in yet another way. I learnt to keep a lot about myself hidden because I didn't want to be alienated from this group of friends. If I did, I would be alone again. I could not stand the thought of that but it began to happen slowly anyway.

Chapter 9

That Social God Called Alcohol and Sitting on the Rock

As time went on, my friends were less interested in spiritual affairs or saving the world and more interested in music, surfing and the physical attractions that they began to feel for one another. I was the same, but I missed how things had been. I craved at times to talk about something deeper than just "things". I was even more confused as I struggled with my own identity. I did begin to understand that what you wore definitely affected how people treated you. I learnt that to be fashionable meant wolf whistles and compliments from people instead of the abuse that Rose and I had suffered when we walked around in baggy jeans and flannelette shirts.

I found that I had to give up some of my ideals in order to keep up with my friends as we became young men and women in the seventies. I also found that I no longer enjoyed my wonderful relationship with my parents as I felt that I had to fight wildly with them, for even the slightest freedom to venture with my friends past the beach and our downstairs room. It had taken weeks of arguing to even be allowed that freedom. I could understand why they were worried, after all I couldn't even swim, and they had been through hell worrying about me in the past, so I knew that they did not want to worry anymore.

However, when I was fourteen and still pleading to go, I really dug my heels in until eventually my father convinced mum to relax enough to allow me to live as a normal teenager. My poor mother found this very difficult as she had completely cared for and protected me, far beyond the normal span of complete care that mothers were required to give. For this reason mum found it even harder to let go and allow her daughter to take risks of any kind.

As I began to feel attracted to the opposite sex in a non-academic way, my mother reeled in horror. Mum saw this behaviour of wanting to date boys before the age of twenty one, as being totally immoral. It was nothing short of walking the path to hell and my mother could not accept that this was normal behaviour for a teenager of the seventies, or any other age for this matter. She couldn't understand how her devoted catholic daughter could suddenly turn into "a dog on heat", a hussy and a common tart as mum so often called me over those turbulent times. Mum used these names whenever she discovered an offending diary entry, or worse still the day she found the contraceptive pill in my bedroom. My mother and I fought bitterly.

I was naive and believed that every time I felt that wild rush of hormones associated with teenage mutual attractions, it was a sign of pure love and it would most certainly end in marriage. Needless to say, during those tumultuous teenage years this was never the case and as each romance ended I would feel as if the end of my world had occurred. Each time it happened, I always blamed it on my inadequacies even if I was the one that had ended it. Like any teenager, I found this time to be the beginning of wild confusion. I did not understand how I could forget the ideals and rules that I had made for myself just so I could fit in with my friends that did nothing for the state of our planet, let alone my small family.

It was also the time that I began to form my own adult relationship with my father who had always stayed my hero. My father and I would have philosophical talks about life and the problems in society. This usually happened when dad had a few too many drinks of alcohol, as that was when he was relaxed and talkative. Sometimes we would drive my mother crazy by talking about dropping out of society and becoming hippies that lived in the bush and were completely self-sufficient. Once, this discussion even involved a plan to grow marijuana as a source of enlightenment and income. My friends and I had started smoking marijuana when we finished our junior high school years. This was very much an accepted part of our surfing culture, but most of our parents could never accept it.

My parents made their sober thoughts on the subject perfectly clear, when I mistakenly talked about the topic when they hadn't been drinking. They told me to tell them if I was smoking the stuff so that they could ring the police immediately, if I said that I was.

Luckily they told me this in one shocked statement, so for the first time I was able to lie and so save myself from being arrested. I was shocked at my parent's reaction to something that we had already talked about and I vowed that I would never again confide in them completely. This made me sad.

My early experiments with marijuana were nondescript and then paranoia followed, until I got used to its effects. We enjoyed the idea of getting stoned and hanging out listening to music.

This could only happen at my place when there was no chance of my parents being at home. We had made a new friend. He lived on the bluff overlooking the ocean. His parents were university lecturers and more importantly to us they were hippies who did not see smoking pot as a criminal activity. We could relax here and have band practice. I thought those days were fantastic. Eventually, the company that I found myself in and the effects of smoking marijuana brought with it some kind of spiritual experience. For me, it was almost like *that* feeling. It created a new way of communicating with that feeling and even better it blocked out the raging torrent of thoughts fed by anxiety, fear and total confusion that seemed to be part of everything I experienced.

My parents argued bitterly but they also taught values that I appreciated even as a rebellious teenager. My father instilled in me two simple ones by which he lived this life.

"To thine own self be true" was perhaps the most important one that I learned to live by. He also taught me that you do not give and expect something in return, as this will only lead you to bitter disappointment.

He would sometimes say that "He who is without sin can cast the first stone," whenever mum or I would start criticising other people.

When I asked him what he meant, I saw how this saying suited lots of occasions. I firmly believed in these values and I lived accordingly. I also believed very strongly that all people are created equal, and should be treated that way.

I was fascinated by how many different types of people there were. I loved to make friends who were different. It was this array of different friends that caused my parents further concern that resulted in fiery confrontations where emotional insults flew like daggers into my heart. Once again, I asked God how people could say that they loved Him, and call themselves Christians, when they said such horrible things. I couldn't understand how my parents brought me up with beliefs that they could not live by. I started to loathe the social activity of drinking alcohol, or at least whenever my parents did it, as it could transform them into monsters. I would often cry myself to sleep as I desperately tried to use my skill of turning words into meaningless sounds. Even if I succeeded in doing this, the sounds still made me sob because they were still so cruel and vicious.

I was no angel either. Like most teenagers, I also experimented with alcohol in my senior high school years. My first experience had been at my grandmother's funeral, in Wollongong. I had been given "a couple of drinks" by my very fashionable aunty and uncle. I was fifteen. I remember becoming quite drunk in the middle of peeling beetroot with my cousin, in their kitchen. I enjoyed the carefree feeling that it gave me and I giggled at the brightly coloured peel falling into the sink, as I tried to control my badly co-coordinated body. I enjoyed how alcohol had transformed me. I didn't behave like a monster. I simply felt warm inside with a confidence that I had lacked since I entered the teenage world where my differences were not only more obvious, but worse still, they had multiplied or so it seemed to me.

Sometimes my friends and I would enjoy drinking around a fire at the beach and once again philosophise on the meaning and purpose of our lives but this time we did it through that other perspective of drunken haze. We also used alcohol to give us false courage and added social "cool' status, before going out to parties. Sometimes drinking alcohol would throw me into my inner universe without any warning. One minute I would be talking to my friends and the next I would feel so tired that I would have to run to find somewhere safe to pass out. Sometimes it would happen so quickly that I would literally fall off my chair, sound asleep. This sleep could last for twenty four hours. However it happened, I always found myself diving deeply into my inner universe at a rapid pace.

I would watch my inner planets and galaxies spin past me at an alarming rate. Finally I would encounter complete darkness, and feel myself cocooned by it. Sometimes I frightened my family and friends because when it happened it was apparently impossible to awaken me until my inner journey was complete, and, as I said that could take up to twenty four hours. Of course this led to even more parental battles and worse still, cruel comments from my peers and even my friends. It seemed more conceivable that the miracle child had become the devil teenager that slept with anyone and trashed friends by leaving them unexpectedly at parties. It was easier to think I somehow "got started" on the drinking before anyone else and so was a disgusting mess, worthy of scorn and not help as I lay unable to move. It was easier to believe all of that than to believe that I had actually been asleep and had some weird reaction to that social god called alcohol. It seemed that a bad reaction to that would be a bigger embarrassment and problem than just being an out of control drunken, immoral teenager.

This also added to my confusion. I was only doing the same as everyone else, yet when I did it, it was nothing like everyone else's experience. My parents drank and turned into monsters. This seemed to be accepted, but even when I was old enough to drink; my parents never seemed to accept me drinking, even though I remained peaceful. I didn't always fall asleep when I drank, and anyway I didn't ever drink that much, yet I was always the one that looked as if I had simply overdosed on the stuff, as I slept through a party.

Yes these high school years were very different. I was no longer the miracle child, but the child who had fallen from grace. The skills that I had used earlier to survive physical pain were now being used to escape a very different kind of pain, which at times felt much worse. This was the pain of hearing harsh criticism from the very people who had always been there to protect me from the very thing that they were now doing.

I became a very angry, sad, young woman.

I was still a top achiever academically, but I felt as though I was scoring rather badly in understanding myself, and other people.

I still loved my school work despite all the new distractions that continually seemed to try to take me away from it.

The time finally came to sit for our final exams. The evening before they were to begin I felt tortured. Although I had studied, I still felt a feeling of impending doom in the shape of failure. I walked down to the beach and sat on my favourite rock. The sun was setting and the surf had a silver shine to it. As I looked out to the horizon and then to the waves crashing on the rocks beneath me. I felt a whisper of that elusive feeling and with it came these thoughts,

"I don't need to worry.

It isn't happening right now.

Now I'm here and the rock that I'm sitting on, the ocean and the sky will all be here eternally.

They will not disappear if I fail.

This will always be here.

The exam won't be.

The ocean will let me return even if I fail.

This will all still be here for me no matter what."

These thoughts lifted all my sense of impending doom. They were replaced by *that* feeling. I even felt a part of everything around me.

I did pass. I came in the first five percent of the state. I was accepted into every university and received every traineeship and scholarship that I had applied for. I decided to accept the dietetics cadetship of which only eight were offered in the entire state. My father was especially thrilled. He shouted everyone that was at the local bowling club, a bottle of champagne when he took my friends and me there to celebrate.

By this time, I also had a boyfriend who was the absolute love of my life. He really was tall dark and incredibly handsome. What made him even more attractive to me was the fact that he shared exactly the same views as me as far as materialism and society went. He had been a rebellious student who left school as soon as he could. I was madly in love with him and this made my parents just mad. They wanted me to fall in love with a doctor or something like that; so that he could look after me should my legs cause me trouble in later life or worse still after childbirth. At least that is how I saw it at the time and for many years to come. This love of my life called Robert was my parent's worst nightmare.

Chapter 10
Dropping Out

When the dust of celebrations settled, I decided to attend a summer school in physics and chemistry at my future university, in Sydney. I stayed with my grandparents as I would when university began. I was excited by the prospect, of spending so much time with them alone. It was going to be a welcome change from clashing with my parents every day.

I walked through those university gates stripped from all my friends support and filled with optimism that I would be surrounded by likeminded souls. I found my class. They were waiting for our lecturer outside our room.

"No one else knows anyone here," I reassured myself as I approached the fashionably dressed group, wearing my hippy clothes and a very nervous smile.

"Hello," I heard myself say. I was deafened by the stony stares and silence, as I quickly retreated into the classroom. The whole two hour session went by with no one except the lecturer speaking to me. I was devastated. On my way home I tried to understand why people weren't all friendly. I felt like a big country bumpkin. I decided that I didn't want to associate with such egotistical people. I wondered what had happened to the university that I had pictured teaming with people who were eager to greet one another as brothers and sisters, united with the desire to transform the world. I guessed this all died in the sixties. I couldn't understand how anything could change with attitudes like the ones that I had met at this university. Their fashion statements were proof enough, I decided.

When I reached my grandparents' house that day, I was miserable. I felt as bad as the times that I was away from my parents, in hospital. No matter what my poor Nar and Pop did, I couldn't stop crying. The next day I felt even more nervous about my classes. The day was exactly as joyless as it had been the day before. I couldn't even concentrate on anything that my teacher said. That night I rang my parents and begged to come home. When my mother arrived, she tried to convince me to stay. I was devastated once more, as she made me go to university the next day. I felt cheated as I did not understand how the same mother that had always wanted to protect me far beyond normal years, could now be forcing me to go it alone in what was to me a hostile environment that made me feel very much like a cripple. When I struggled home that day, I found that my grandmother had convinced her that it was cruel to make me stay.

I was so happy, but my mother was not. Our trip home was silent until three of my close friends, Gibbo, Marilyn and Adam appeared in our carriage. They were returning home from orientation day at their new university. I was disappointed when I learnt that their new university was the one I had just fled from. As moments of doubt began to creep over me, I decided that it wasn't just a horrid feeling of loneliness that had made me leave but also the hypocrisy of it all. After all, I was meant to become a dietician and work for three years in a hospital that I knew for a fact was incapable of ever serving a fresh nutritional meal. I knew this was the case from my long stays in all sorts of hospitals. That was the real reason I dropped out.

Somewhere on that trip home, I also realised that I missed Robert and couldn't bear to be apart from him. I couldn't break his heart by joining in the root of society's problems by studying to qualify for a high paying, hypocritical job, that did nothing but made you consume more than necessary to keep up with the it-crowd.

When I got home Robert dropped me and broke my heart. He told me that he couldn't stop me from getting a good job. He thought that I was doing what I did to make him happy. I was heartbroken. Every choice that I made was done because I believed in it, and I *couldn't* believe that someone that I had loved didn't even know this much about me. Heartbreak was quickly replaced by more anger. I renewed the vow that I would never work in a position that did not contribute to our global, social and environmental wellbeing, no matter how much the pay. This would make choosing a job easy, or so I thought.

Primary school teaching was the only possible choice because a teacher could subtly influence children to see the world in a different way, and, other than in the staff room, you didn't really have to mix with adults. My father did not agree and wanted me to try other things first. He was a teacher and he wanted me to do a lot better than him. I managed to further break Dad's heart by dropping out of every other course that would have led me to a profession that in his eyes would provide me with a brighter future. I dropped out of an Arts degree course at our local university, an electrocardiogram cadetship, and a pathology course, all within one semester.

One job that I loved was working in the new markets selling beanbags. Claire got the job for me, to give me some pocket money whilst I attempted to be a uni- student. Ironically I made more of a career working in the markets than I ever did by going to university. I loved this colourful world of different people from not just all over the world but from every conceivable walk of life: from white witches to a Sydney mayor; Hindus, Sikhs and Jews; black and white, they were all one caring community that travelled between Sydney and Newcastle selling their equally colourful wares. I learnt a lot about life there, and my own self-worth.

Chapter 11

Different Threads

This story could become many different things depending which thread of my life I choose to tease out of the tattered mess that my life had become. Once adulthood dawned, life got a bit messy. I lost track of childhood dreams of who I would be. This happened because I got bombarded with those messages that tell us what, who and how we should be. Any thoughts involving my inner self got drowned out by everything that surrounded me on the outside. Young adults all around the world have jam packed lives. I did too back then. To tell all of it would be a waste of time, because so many dramatic stories of youth have been told. Everyone has their own. It's all been done.

We always want to know what we might have missed out on, so I'll tell you some of the threads of my life that I've chosen to omit. I call them threads because threads are used to make incredible fabrics of every kind. I like to imagine the fabric of this life as lace because nothing is finer, more delicate or more complicated than lace. When you examine each little detail of lacework you see lots of little knots which if seen in any other needlecraft would drive you crazy as you tried to undo them. Instead, in lacework these knots make up the beauty of the entire piece of fabric. This is life. We are driven crazy by obstacles in our life or the knots but often it all works out as we see the bigger picture. This life is a delicate lacework.

Here are the other threads, most of which were filled with the toughest knots and the reason why I left them out of this story. The most obvious one at this point is made up of sex and drugs and rock and roll. This thread would make a story of encounters with rock legends such as Cold Chisel, Angry Anderson, Lou Reed, and Midnight Oil; wild parties in the mansions of rebellious, anti-establishment children held with their wealthy parents' permission and pub scenes from the dawn of the new wave punk era in Sydney. It would all be there. As I said this is boring compared to the unique thread of this story. The endings of these stories are often predictable. Unless you are the star, they often go nowhere.

I left out the hippy communes and I think we all know why. Most of those just ended up with old hippies and no life changing powers ever emerged from them, no matter how many "out of it experiences" brought on by drugs they may have had. Not enough stories have been told about "out of it experiences" that don't involve drugs and if they *are* told then there is generally nothing appealing about them as they usually involve a mental illness or a horrid hallucinogenic experience bought on by a hideous disease or circumstance.

All the beautiful "out of it stories" are usually found in historical documents, dry old religions of the past, or fiction.

I could go down the road of surviving child abuse including horror stories of bashings and rapes committed by family members and so called friends. We see and hear so many of these stories through the media, so at this point in history we need solutions and not more stories.

I could have also made it all about becoming aware of and then battling Australia's racist attitudes towards many people but most of all towards our own Aboriginal people in Redfern in the seventies. This thread will finish weaving its own picture long after this book ends. The picture of this thread deserves to be framed in a separate story.

This book could also become a self-help book about overcoming a physical disability, but there are remarkable ones already told. If it became this story then only those who have been labelled disabled would read it. The fact is that so many people have told their incredible stories of overcoming far worse physical disabilities.

Sometimes the real hidden disability that has to be overcome is fear. Fear can cripple anyone. From my personal experience all the caring doctors, friends and relatives were so focused on fixing my obvious disability that they missed my biggest one. I might have walked but I was incapable of holding my head up because I was petrified of what I had learnt about life. Everyone knows that you don't get very far if you can't see ahead of you.

I am going to follow the thread that tells a story of very strong inner experiences that were brought on by nothing except remembering the search for *that* childhood feeling and deciding to follow this thread that connected me to it. It led me to fulfil every childhood goal no matter how far-fetched it seemed and to overcome every disability. This connection was so thin that it was like a fine silk thread that just floated almost invisibly in the breeze but then at times it became a strong presence in my life as it twisted and turned until it became a piece of incredibly fine but strong lacework that demanded attention. When this thread was directed the big picture was the most incredibly beautiful piece of lacework in the fabric my life.

The search for that feeling led me to hold the very hand that tatters that thread into this lacework and it runs in everyone's life. This story may be unique now because one like it has never been told in these modern times but it will not stay this way. It will become just one of countless stories. It will be the story of all of us. It is the story of our evolution that is continually occurring.

The entire planet can feel that there is something; a whisper of something both more than us and of more to us. If this isn't the truth then why have we accepted angels, spirit guides, psychics, tarot readers, astrology and an endless array of new age products. This millennium they are a part of life but in the last one they were all seen as almost the curse of society. The time is right for us to connect to a fourth dimension that *is* reality. The thread of this story will take you there.

This story isn't something to believe in or to imagine but one that you can truly experience.

It has a magic that is real and ready for you to discover.

The thread I have chosen delved into my very core and healed every possible hidden wound or flaw without me even knowing it.

I've chosen this divine thread in the tatter of my life to weave this story because it is different.

It is the universal truth.

It isn't just a "me" story, although I do have to tell it in the context of my life.

It is about an ancient part of all of us that has been dormant since childhood but whispering to us to stir it into action. Just by re-reading parts of what is to follow you can begin your own unique story in a dimension you never knew existed.

Another reason for telling this thread is because it is proof that miracles are real and just waiting for all of us.

Now back to the story. Life was confusing. Outside I was the absolutely typical disillusioned angst ridden youth. Inside I was now almost crippled.

Chapter 12

Gibbo, Rosary Beads and a Chain around My Neck

As I was becoming enlightened, my parents' mood was darkening. They did not approve of my new friends who were very anti-establishment. To me, these were people prepared to turn their back on materialism because they could see it was leading the world to imminent destruction. To my parents and probably the rest of the world, they were a pack of shabby, drug dazed people whose lack of material possessions was more a result of their inability to work, rather than any political statement.

I must admit, I quickly began to enjoy the path to enlightenment via drug induced discussions and music, rather than any more praying. Once I dropped out of my last course, I was free to live like a gypsy following the markets to work in Paddy's market and Flemington as well as Newcastle. When I worked in Sydney, I lived with a collection of older hippies, including a black belt in martial arts, and a 7ft bisexual eccentric. The only person that was my age was my new friend Zara who designed clothes for Madam Lash and a punk band called Jimmy and the Boys. They were so different to my old friends that had waited to talk to Mary with me, in my younger days.

Eventually I left home behind and lived with the collection of hippies. I felt rather proud of this accomplishment as I had not just learnt to walk but I had flown the nest dragging my crippled emotional self with me. I even managed to survive the city that had sent me home in tears little than a year ago, and I was mixing with people that I had only read about or seen in movies. I had often bawled to my mother that I could not stand the "Newcastle mentality". It was boring and people didn't understand me. I would rant about this after an end of the world scenario involving bitchy schoolgirls or the love of my life that always left me. Here in this new world I had created, people did understand me and not only that, they really respected me and protected me from own naivety.

While I explored the world of markets, my old friends pursued their academic careers.

Marilyn and Gibbo eventually escaped university dorm life and shared a house with other students. Gibbo and I renewed our friendship. He had not only stayed true to his catholic religion but also managed to include some very different practices, such as meditation and even knowledge about chakras. He still went to church, but he told me that his most powerful prayers were uttered in a special place on the rocks at the local beach. He loved Mary too and his love for her had grown. He liked to pray to her and meditate in this special place. His favourite prayer was the "Hail Mary." One night he showed me this place and how to meditate. It was simple. We said the Hail Mary and then tried not to think.

This brought a taste of *that* feeling. There was nothing except the endless sound of the ocean.

The breeze seemed to stroke my cheeks and I truly felt I was a part of everywhere and with everything. We sat on that rock in eternal silence. We opened our eyes and looked at each other at the same time and kept our silence until we reached the car. I was still savouring the experience of finding that long lost and almost forgotten feeling when Gibbo started both the engine and his account of how he had once managed to open his third eye. This quickly got my thoughts restarted as I didn't know what he could possibly be talking about. I had never heard of such a thing existing except on the forehead of monsters in bad horror movies. I did not know whether to be impressed or sympathetic.

Gibbo explained that this was a chakra that was situated between our actual eyes. He said that Buddha had opened it. I might have turned against our church but some of its rules I did still hold sacred, especially the one about not worshipping false gods. From my limited knowledge I considered that Buddha could very well be one of these gods, but Gibbo was such a religious *and* intelligent person that he wouldn't do anything so stupid as to break such holy laws. After all he was studying medicine.

Gibbo told me that one night his third eye opened and it gave him the ability to see in the dark. He even told me that he could walk through the bush without either moonlight or a torch to guide him and he was able to see everything that lay on the track in front of him. It wasn't this unbelievable story that had the greatest impact on me. It was one simple concluding sentence.

That simple sentence was, "I started to think about what was happening and straight away I stumbled over and I couldn't see anymore."

I didn't say anything in response. I just enjoyed this moment as I thought how Gibbo's story reminded me of my childhood game of making words become just sounds by not thinking about their meaning. Teenage years had nearly erased this concept, as words were too heavy with meaning. He had also rekindled my love for Mary. I had definitely forgotten about this. All my passion had been diverted from religious pursuits to being a rebellious, "greenie" teenager of the seventies.

I enjoyed this feeling so much that when I returned home I took to wearing my silver rosary beads around my neck. This was long before Madonna had made wearing them a fashion statement. I savoured life's own high too much to cloud it with drugs or alcohol, so I gave them up. I even tried out Gibbo's meditation. When I did this, I felt myself becoming incredibly light, as I had been in my dreams of flying. I could feel Gibbo's special place. I could tell Gibbo was there. It was so real. I could almost taste the salt. I didn't stop meditating - *it* just stopped. I looked at the time and went to bed.

Next time I saw Gibbo, he looked at me with a twinkle that only Gibbo had, and stunned me once again in a single sentence, "Long distance phone call without the phone," and smiled.

I don't remember what I said. I just remember that I understood.

At the time of this return to religion, my flatmates were so impressed with my ability to abstain from anything mind-altering that they began to treat me as *their* miracle child. This was very flattering except that it took me away from my meditations and made me put away the rosaries forever. My friend's flattery became a chain around my neck as they began to react like my parents if they even thought I was going to have a drink or a smoke.

I rebelled against them just as I had my parents and pursued my old ways of enlightenment usually by smoking some kind of mind altering substance or enjoying honey saturated in the juice of magic mushrooms.

I chose to resume this way because nearly everyone that I knew did it, and I was tired of being different. I just wanted to be normal and not special anymore. I justified this fall from grace to my friends, by insisting that I had to try more drugs in order to have an informed opinion on this controversial pastime. I'd be a hypocrite if I hadn't tried out all their addictions. This way I could understand them and even help them, as I still managed to save people from time to time, like the junkie who passed out with a needle in his arm at the local shop. People there helped me to take him home for Christmas. I couldn't do this if I didn't understand his high and his craving for it. I'd just see him as a derelict street kid and leave it at that. If you could change one person, then maybe you could fix the world, someone famous had once said. I made all these points to my friends and promised that I would go to college the following year to be a teacher and try to change some children instead of the world.

I still went home to see my family. My little hometown took on a new beauty, now that I had something to compare it to. I marvelled at just how beautiful the Norfolk pines were that lined the street to the beach and I enjoyed star gazing from our verandah at night as the lights of Sydney made this impossible there. I always looked forward to catching up with a few of my old friends that had remained loyal to all our teenage discussions. The person whose company I missed the most when I was in Sydney was my dear little sister. We had had our ups and downs during these turbulent times but Madeline was always glad to see me come home. The absolute highlight of these visits was seeing her.

We loved partying together through long summer nights. My friends still enjoyed the odd joint. One night we all tried tripping with LSD. As usual I saw it as a chance for more enlightenment, or perhaps some enlightenment. I took it and went for a walk to the beach. I remember looking at the moonlit water as though I had never seen it before. It was incredible. It seemed as though the moonlight was liquid silver dancing on the surface.

My body did not feel at all incredible. As a matter of fact, I felt like I wasn't in my own body at all. I didn't have an out of body experience. Instead, I felt like I was inside of another body that was too short with feet that were enormous and could not possibly be mine. I reminded myself that no matter what enlightenment I may have been receiving I had also taken a very strong drug. I decided to just sit down and enjoy where I was, as it was too difficult to use those gigantic feet, not to mention the shoes that seemed to drag along the ground when I carried them.

I was facing the mighty red cliff that gives Redhead its name, when suddenly it was eerily lit and before my astounded eyes, Aboriginal drawings appeared on the rock face. The sound of didgeridoos and rhythm sticks began to fill my head. Next came the most beautiful singing and then they appeared in front of me. The Aboriginals that once lived here were dancing their ancestral dance. They had returned to their sacred place. I was stunned. I knew that they were not really there but I was watching them. I just put it down to the effects of a rather remarkable drug that allowed you to see the things that you were so deeply interested in that you didn't even know it. That night at the beach was a very special moment, but it made me forget all about *that* feeling of meditating with Gibbo. We lost track of each other.

When I did see Gibbo again, it was unexpected and back in Newcastle. He managed to create another special moment that had whispers of that feeling but I didn't understand it. I was standing in my kitchen, cigarette in hand and stoned as was now usual, with aggressive new age music blaring and my odd assortment of punk and hippie flatmates. I turned as I heard people coming into the house and there he was. He looked at me with a flicker of disappointment. I remember only one sentence again. It stood out because I couldn't really understand it.

I understood the words, but Gibbo's twinkle stirred something deep inside of me as he said,

"You can't give up smoking until you find something to replace it."

I just knew he wasn't talking about the obvious replacements of food, knitting, or walking, but I didn't understand. I remember choosing to leave it that way. I left a lot of things in that moment without even realising it. It was the last time I saw Gibbo for decades.

Chapter 13

Redhead to Redfern

I kept my promise and started training to be a primary schoolteacher. I knew what an impact my teachers had on me but I would not be a teacher like the ones that taught through sheer terror. This profession let me spend less time with adults and this was a plus because I enjoyed children's company much more than most adults. I attempted to move back home, but the dreaded Newcastle mentality was alive and kicking, as was my parents' drunken abuse and disapproval of how I chose my friends.

During my first year of college I managed to rescue a starving, abused horse from being put down by adopting him despite the fact I only knew about horses from books and had only ridden on family holidays. It had always been a dream to own one and I decided that rather than own a car I would travel by horse so as not to pollute the planet or to waste precious petrol. It all made perfect sense to me.

Living at home proved to be as impossible as keeping a gelding in your front yard of suburbia. The horse and I both, moved on to what we thought were greener grasses. In my horse's case this was true but mine was debateable. I moved from Redhead to Redfern. Redfern was an inner city area, seething with social problems and black activists that I knew nothing about. My little village had shielded me from these harsh realities of life. As a matter of fact I knew little about life in general. I had no idea that divisions of class even existed in our country.

When a sociology lecturer explained to my class that teachers should expect less educational outcomes from students living in low socio economic areas such as Redfern, I was stunned and indignant. I hadn't even realised that I was living in an area with such a label. Once I digested this news, I fearlessly pointed out to this lecturer that Redfern wasn't a hot bed of problems where people did not achieve academically, as I lived there and that meant there must be dozens like me.

Just as Redhead and Redfern were two towns that were the opposite of each other, the girlfriend that I moved with became the total opposite to all I thought I knew her to be. Her long flowing hippie locks had been shorn to a punk hairstyle, her lace shawls and flowing dresses were replaced by singlet tops and old army pants. Her long earrings were replaced by numerous studs including one in her nose. Remember this was the seventies and body piercings still scared people.

Punks and mods made up the music scene that I found myself living in the thick of. It was so much more hard core than the one in Newcastle. I never imagined that Sydney, my city of miracles had so many hidden worlds to it, but I quickly adjusted.

The houses that I lived in were all occupied by musicians. They were completely opposite to the ones I had been used to. These were loud, angry pioneering musicians that experimented in all forms of distortion. This distortion was in their lyrics, the sounds of their home made electric guitars and the way they lived their lives each day.

I paid my way through college with a scholarship and by selling fairy floss at Luna Park.

I enjoyed my job but I stopped work with a sudden jolt one morning. I woke with *that* feeling that only lingered after one of *those* dreams. In this dream I was working at the park as usual. There were the usual crowds and queues. The Ghost train had its usual long line of customers, but in the dream I focussed on this queue, to see flashes of people screaming as a fire licked the walls of horror inside the ride. I had never been on this ride, but I knew that it was a very real dream. It even reminded me of the childhood one with bursting balloons. My flatmates knew about my premonitions. I told them that I might have been mad but I had to opt for poverty and quit. They quickly reassured me that in my case it was not madness. Instead of working my shift later that day, I went and handed in my uniforms and quit immediately.

It was the next shift that the Ghost Train caught fire. It was my shift. The shift I had been rostered on. People were seriously injured, some fatally. I had had one of those dreams again and I didn't particularly enjoy it. I could not believe that those dreams were back.

Fortunately the demands of college were too hectic to dwell on any of this for long. In my last year of college I moved to a flat above a Korean deli and a Laundromat in Redfern Street. Across the road were Redfern Courthouse and the Catholic Church with its adjoining presbytery. The priest at this church was different. It was obvious that he was not materialistic because he had given his presbytery to the local homeless, Aboriginal people. At night they would light a fire and sit around it drinking and singing while someone played the guitar. During the day they would just stand around on the footpath talking.

I dared to break the unspoken white Australian rule back then and I crossed the road to mix with them to understand how these third world scenes had come to be a part of their lives. I even visited the Eveleigh Street, or The Block as it was known without even realising that whites never went there. I felt as though I had stepped into a third world country, as I walked past burnt out cars that were used to block the road to stop police cars from entering it. Barefoot children froze in their game of ball and looked at me as though I was from Mars.

I had been shocked to learn of our true history but I was even more shocked to see its aftermath that was still alive here in Redfern but kept so secret. That moment on Redhead beach flashed through my mind. It seemed odd to be seeing all this less than twelve months after that incredible LSD fuelled moment that was shared with ancient Aboriginals. The drug had shown me a glimpse of what was truly an unknown, deep passion that would become a major part of my future. This one moment standing in Eveleigh Street and remembering was the beginning of this future that belongs in another book. I didn't know that either.

I didn't always mix with the down and out. My new flatmates were all relatively conservative with full time jobs. I had another circle of friends that included Indonesians, Maoris, Timorese, Balinese, Cook Islanders and Aboriginals as well as Europeans from different countries.

One night I invited our non-white friends back home after we had all enjoyed a night together at the pub. My white flatmates were disgusted and told me that I could mix with this "shit" when we were out but I could not go inviting it into our home.

Needless to say I asked these friends to move on - not just out of my home but out of my life. I was mortified that people I had shared my life with could have this vile attitude.

I saw everything in black and white at the time, so if you didn't treat all people equally, and follow my other beliefs, then you were no longer in my circle of friends. Sure I'd be prepared to discuss the issues, but if you dared to think I was wrong, then that was the finish, as time was too short to waste on people who were a part of the world's problems and not a part of possible solutions. I didn't even notice it when friends disappeared from my life. There was no time.

I had graduated from college before my flatmates left. I thought back to the moment I had told my father that I was dropping out of all studies to have a break. The look on Dad's face as he told me that I would never do anything if I took that break, had every fear that he held for my future etched into it. In that moment I secretly vowed that I would prove my dad to be wrong.

I had proved him wrong and best of all I had done it without asking my parents for a cent. I had for once in my life stood on my own two feet in a positive way. I reminded Dad of what he had said and he grinned. He gave me the biggest hug as he told me he was proud of me. My mother and sister were too. It was written all over their faces. This was the first time I had seen this expression for a very long time and it felt fantastic.

When I came home from graduation, my flatmate who fancied himself as a yogi and a bit of a psychic, congratulated me and then made what I found to be a totally stupid statement, not to mention inappropriate and totally random.

He announced, "23, hey! You'll be married by the time you are 24."

My elevated mood dropped dramatically, and I quickly denied such a prediction, telling my poor friend in no uncertain terms, that

I would never have children as the world was going to end anyway and I would never be so irresponsible as to marry. All the time I was passionately making my declaration every fibre of my being seemed to be screaming silently to me that he was absolutely correct. Like so many other things, this baffled me and happened in an instant.

I started casual teaching in the local schools. City kids had scared me, so I decided to start out working with them so that when I got a permanent job I would be prepared for anything. I fell in love with my inner city teaching life.

The racist flatmates left and the friends that had been invited home after the pub that night, moved in. At least these friends were not at all materialistic and all were exactly who they appeared to be. Best of all none of them knew me as the crippled kid, miracle child or wild child. They all respected me as an equal. They just accepted me as I was.

We spent times together that were reminiscent of the days spent in the down stairs room at home. I had learnt to keep my mission to help change the world a little more secret with the exception of those drunken conversations when we focused on all the deep and meaningfuls and attempted to solve all the world's problems. No one ever remembered these conversations so my secret cause was safe.

The joy of having multicultural friends subsided when I decided that it was time I introduced them to my friends and family in Redhead, as one of these friends had blossomed into my fiancé. I was excited at the thought of coming home with my news. We headed straight to the local club when we arrived in Redhead as it was Friday night and just about everyone in town would be there, including my parents.

My parents' face turned from surprise at seeing me to horror at who I'd arrived with.

My best friends came out with the most shocking statement, "But Lisa they are black!"

One friend questioned me about sexual myths regarding black people. Most of them whispered racist jokes to me. I was astounded and so hurt. I had never known people even thought that way. Pure shock kept me calm. Later, I learnt that this horrid reaction was prejudice and racism. The only reason I had never known that this hideous thing existed in my hometown was because there simply were no coloured people living anywhere near it.

I hadn't even noticed that my friends were "black" or "coloured." They weren't anyway. They were all the shades of brown that all of us white Aussies tried to turn each summer.

When my fiancé, Dan a beautiful Cook Islander, asked my parents for their permission to marry we were horrified when my father refused. I gave the speech about God creating all men equal and that you shouldn't preach what you can't practise. My father gave the one of disownment if I continued my plan for the future. I continued the plan.

Chapter 14

Wedded Bliss, Tanaya and Meeting My Hero

Gradually, the shock of those reactions to our good news wore off and I got used to being "disowned." Dan and I loved each other and that was all that mattered. We began to make our wedding plans.

My parents eventually had a change of heart.

They had asked each other if they would have taken any notice of their parents if they tried to stop *them* from marrying and the answer was a deafening "No".

As a result we all went from not speaking, to arguing over hire cars. Dad had insisted that he would pay for these and we insisted that it was a waste of money. Finally, Dad agreed to grant our wish and let us arrive in the family car driven by my uncle. We would marry in August, 1982. I was twenty four, but I didn't remember my friend's prediction. I only knew about love and all it entailed.

At least our marriage plans brought a positive reaction from the Redfern community. Apparently it had been years since anyone had ever married in Redfern, never mind in the church where all the homeless Aboriginals gathered. The local people were moved as we chose their businesses to provide all that was needed for a traditional yet simple wedding. It felt as though everyone that had a part in the organisation became family.

Our wedding day finally came and I did not have a hint of pre wedding jitters.

There was only one strange moment before the wedding and that was when we stopped at the lights on Moore Park Rd and I looked out at the green space.

Out of nowhere came the thought, "This does not mean forever. It isn't like the ocean. It can be changed."

This thought shocked me. I loved Danny deeply and this love had been enough to make me forget all about the impending doom of the planet. I no longer wanted to pledge my life to one of childless devotion to the cause. All I wanted was to pledge my life to this man. I was going to take the ultimate step and not just marry, but marry in my faith. I wasn't joining forces with the hypocrites, as I'd called its followers, because through living in Redfern I had found a priest that was true to every word that Christ had uttered. He hadn't just given his presbytery to the homeless Aboriginals but he always made them welcome to come inside the church at any time and join in or ask for money or whatever their need may be.

This priest did not judge. He just loved, respected and helped. He didn't make us jump through religious hoops to be able to marry as Dan was not a catholic. He just asked if Dan believed in God and would he support me in my beliefs. Dan agreed and I knew he meant it as we had discussed all types of spiritual affairs including my religion. I was taking a solemn vow for eternity and I loved Dan completely.

The ceremony was unique. Homeless aboriginals asked my middle class relatives for money or cigarettes as they arrived at the church. Mum Shirl, a well-known Aboriginal activist rallied up a small choir to sing songs that Dan and I had chosen. The priest known as Fighting Father Ted Kennedy burst into applause as soon as he had finished declaring us husband and wife. My relatives thought that they had been tricked into coming to a church of some other weird religion because they did not know that you could do any of this in a Catholic church. They had to be quietly reassured during the ceremony. All the South Sydney supporters cheered as they passed us in front of the church on the way home from their win at Redfern Oval.

Our reception was held in a cosy room upstairs in our local pub. The hotel staff waited on us for free, and gave us silver goblets complete with our names engraved on each one as a wedding present. Our parents were happily served until the early hours of the morning and were the last to leave.

It was a truly special night where everyone forgot colour, race, religion and bank balances and simply enjoyed each other.

Our marriage began perfectly. Now I felt special but in a very normal way, as this was expected of every new bride. That was what made it so special. I had managed to reach a major milestone at the right time of life and in the normal way. We still had the excitement of our single life but within the security of marriage. Dan worked as a storeman for a record company. The pay was not the best but the reward system made up for that. Free records, alcohol and seafood were the regular rewards for hard work. Cheap concert tickets in good seats and invitations to exclusive promotions nights were part of the deal for all workers and their partners. Dan was popular and also the only married man on its staff. All this made our social calendar very busy.

We didn't make the usual newlywed plans of owning a home but we did make our first long term plan and that was to travel. Dan wanted to see all of Australia before we set our sights on any overseas destinations. This sounded like a great plan to me especially the first part as I was petrified at the thought of flying. I even believed that this fear was natural because no one was meant to fly anyway and all jet setting was only consumerism at its worst. I had always staunchly defended my petrified opinion, but I couldn't now that I was married and in love. I learnt that married life created its own world where my previous black and white perceptions took on a more colourful hue. This was a good example. I still held firm my view on jet setting and I was still scared stiff of flying but now flying would mean meeting the rest of Danny's family in New Zealand or sharing exotic experiences with someone that I loved and who would be my legs if I needed! I even liked the idea of seeing more of this global family of which I believed we were all a part.

We agreed that children would have to wait for at least four years, and in the meantime, I would visit a specialist to be sure that I could even have children. Mum had always warned me that perhaps I would find childbirth impossible or perhaps worse still, it would put me in a wheel chair permanently. Dan and I had talked about all these possibilities before talking marriage and we had both decided only one thing mattered- that we would be together. There was no reason for us to deserve the worst anyway.

I saw the specialist in the first few weeks of our marriage. The specialist told me that I was fully capable of falling pregnant and giving birth successfully. His only advice was to give my body a break from the contraceptive pill, as it was a strong dosage. Overjoyed with the unexpected clean bill of gynaecological health, I decided to take his advice and have a break immediately. At last I thought, and when it matters the most, I got results from a doctor saying I was really normal. I'd have kids just like everyone else after all. Yes, in this more protected world of marriage there were many more possibilities.

When December came around we all decided to throw in and have an all weekend Sagittarian birthday party, as six of us had birthdays within the first few days of December. We had the usual wild time with would-be musicians, old friends, great food and of course plenty to drink, and smoke.

When Danny and I returned home early Sunday morning we went to bed, made blissful love and fell into a sound sleep. I remember waking suddenly with that feeling. In a flash I remembered that in my dream, a little baby had told me that it was going to arrive. I quickly buried this thought as it was too real and not at all what we had planned.

By the end of January I was busy throwing up with all-day-sickness. Poor Danny went white when I came out of the doctor's to tell him of the positive pregnancy test. I was devastated. What use where so called specialists I thought, when the things that they are forever telling you will never happen, are the only things that do.

We both recovered from the shock and realised just how lucky we were when my friend's mum gave me a tiny pair of lemon booties. We couldn't wait for our new arrival to fill those little things from that moment on. I refused to go to any pre-natal classes. I was afraid that they would stir old childhood hospital horrors that would put me off ever going there to give birth. I was all for natural things, but I wanted to give birth naturally surrounded by all the drugs and technology should nature fail to take its course. I chose to prepare myself for the ordeal of giving birth by reading.

One night I dreamt that I was holding up a little baby girl with almond eyes as brown as her dad's and thick dark hair. I was calling her "our little Tanaya" and showing her to her dad. This was a name we had discussed but by no means agreed on. I also dreamt of losing her in the bedclothes. I came into the room expecting to see Danny nursing her but he had gone and I could hear the baby crying but couldn't find her amongst the bedclothes.

You guessed it, both these dreams had more than a whisper of *that* feeling but I ignored it all, as life was great. I was teaching at Newtown public school and was popular with all the children who improved both academically and socially while I worked with them. I loved my life each day and I didn't need to pay any attention to any glimpses of the future.

The first day of spring arrived with me rushing to our outside toilet, cursing the packet of chocolate biscuits I had devoured the night before. As I sat on that toilet I noticed a daisy cheekily peeking through a crack and growing in a bed of cement. I stopped cursing and smiled as I realised that it was the first day of spring and how lucky I was to have this precious strong daisy in my cement patch. I admired it again in a couple of hours as I returned to the toilet. On my next visit to the daisy I realised that my chocolate cramps were coming with regularity and increasing strength. By the time I hailed a cab and made it to the hospital, our baby's head was showing and by the time poor Danny got there I was throwing up in the final stage of labour. Before I needed unnatural assistance, I gave birth to a beautiful baby girl that was straight out of my dream.

Before I knew it, I was sobbing with joy and disbelief, telling Danny just as I did in the dream, "Look Danny! It's our little Tanaya!"

Danny seemed a little stunned at my announcement of a name that we hadn't officially agreed on, but when I told him why, he agreed that this had to her name.

When the nurse took Tanaya to check that she was as perfect as she appeared, she made a statement that was most incredible, "You must play a lot of sport as your contractions were so strong."

I had delivered Tanaya easily, but I didn't think it had anything to do with me, as much as my child's eagerness to meet with the world. When Tanaya returned, I was in my room.

This nurse continued the shock process as she entered with a colleague, by declaring,

"Here she is - the one that has made liars out of all of us. She didn't attend one pre-natal class, and she had the best labour and delivery out of everyone."

It seemed I made liars out of most specialists. I smiled.

I left hospital on the fifth day; just as all normal new mothers did. I introduced Tanaya to her new home as if she was royalty. I showed her each and every room talking to her as if she were an adult, explaining what we did in each room and what each large mysterious object was used for. I didn't see Tanaya as our child whose future we had to mould. Instead I saw our role as caretakers of a precious person that had the right to be whatever they were meant or wanted to be, giving a daily dose of unconditional love and truth along the way. Danny was a devoted husband and father. My life was like all the best girls' books I'd ever read.

Money was tight, but we had saved enough to take Tanaya to New Zealand to meet the rest of her family. This money was sacred as we knew we could never save that amount again now that I had stopped working. We made our trip when Tanaya was three months old. I was still petrified at the thought of flying and went every shade of green possible just waiting to take off, never mind when we did. Passengers were kindly offering Dan air sick pills, thinking that I had forgotten to take mine. He thanked them and explained that I was just scared as I'd never flown before.

The flight went well except for the feeling of travelling down a pot holed road which apparently everyone else knew was turbulence and when I nearly died from heart failure as Dan had forgotten to tell me just how close to the coast the airport was, so as everyone else was excitedly looking down at our approach to the city, I was almost screaming in terror, preparing for the crash into the ocean. I never even liked the height of most look outs. This was too much. I begged Dan to stay in New Zealand for a couple of years with his family, when it came time to leave. This was not just because I enjoyed his family so much but also because I was too scared to fly home. I thought perhaps by then a bridge may have been built between the two countries.

Of course, we flew home.

Dan remained the devoted husband and father but I had become only a devoted mother. This, plus financial pressure caused poor Dan to stay that bit longer at every event after work that he still enjoyed. This in turn, made me feel cheated as I was no longer able to see my friends, or earn my own money. None of this would have mattered if Dan had just spent more time with me.

The very thing I craved for I was pushing away by demanding it louder and louder. I thought that Tanaya would be enough to make Dan come running home every day and to not stay away any longer than his job required. This led to arguments fired by his rum and my bourbon, while Tanaya slept innocently.

We seemed to live in heaven or hell with nothing in between. Eventually Dan agreed that I should go back to casual teaching so that we could relieve at least the financial pressure from our marriage. It did this but it created new pressures as I tried to cope with work, feelings of guilt for leaving Tanaya, and the frustration of Dan's and my new inability to talk about our problems.

At this point in time, I began to have that worst possible effect of childbirth, come true. The one my mother had always predicted as a reason for marrying for money. My legs began to give way and cause me to crumple to the ground, like a puppet whose strings had been cut. At my worst, I fell over thirteen times in one day. They weren't dramatic falls, as I learnt to fall gracefully and to pop up again before anyone had time to really tell what had happened. Some falls were dramatic but thankfully they usually occurred alone when rushing to collect Tanaya. I also began to experience strange sensations, as if someone had poured hot water down my leg and into my shoe. I had pains where the pins and plates would grind on my shin. We decided that I had to face the inevitable and find out exactly what was going on, as if we couldn't guess.

My doctor quickly referred me to a specialist whose diagnosis was cruelly simple. "What else do you expect with legs like yours? It is all a part of your condition; you should know this by this stage".

I fought back the tears as I rushed from his room. No I didn't know it was a part of my condition. I had had no idea what my condition had been. I'd only just found out that the little pins that

I had been told held my shin in place as a child, were actually large screws complete with the thread that not just went through a metal plate about 10 centimetres long, but straight through my shin bone and out the other side, and there were not six of them but eight. I obviously knew nothing about "my condition", but I decided to find out.

I found Doctor Colvin's phone number in the book when I got home. I rang and his secretary answered. I explained my plight and asked if I could see the doctor since he understood my problem. She answered that he had had a stroke and no longer took any new patients. I begged her. I explained that if I did not get to see him I would never know what happened to my legs or why. She asked my name and then told me to hold. When she returned she had the answer I wanted. Doctor Colvin would see me as long as I got a referral from my doctor.

I'll never forget sitting in his waiting room. It was exactly as it was when I walked out for the last time as a twelve year old girl. It just seemed a much smaller room. It was tiny as a matter of fact. The leather lounge was still there although not as shiny and the ornate brass lamp that had seemed as if it had come straight from Aladdin's cave, when I was a child, was still sitting on the small table. I heard a cough come from his surgery. The receptionist quickly asked if he was alright. I heard the voice of my hero, although not quite as strong and every hair on my body stood up as I tingled with the excitement of seeing this man again.

"At last," I thought, "I can tell him face to face that he was my hero and that whenever I was asked that teenage question of who is your hero, I would always tell them with pride that I had a real one-a knight called Sir Gordon Colvin because he rescued me from being a cripple."

I forgot about my new leg problem. I just wanted to tell him this. His receptionist entered and brought me back from childhood memories as she told me that since the stroke, Dr Colvin found it difficult to swallow at times. This quickly bought me into the reality that my hero was now a frail old man in his seventies, who saw few patients at all.

I was called to his room and there he stood. He was not seven foot tall but very short. He looked his age and when he went to walk to his chair, after greeting me, I was shocked to see that his stroke had left one leg almost paralysed. I couldn't believe that a man that should have been knighted for all the pioneering work that he had done for his patients so that they could walk, should end up almost a cripple himself.

We sat opposite each other and smiled. He told me that he was ok as he must have read the degree of concern on my face. He explained that he had the stroke as a result of a simple freak accident in his own driveway. He asked me how my father was and if his back was OK. I couldn't believe this either. After more than twenty years, he remembered my dad and his bad back. He asked me what I did as a job. When I told him I was a primary schoolteacher, he just shook his head and smiled, telling me that this was the last thing he would have expected me to do because of the amount of time that teachers spend on their legs.

I smiled and told him how much I loved to be on my legs because I was never meant to be on them at all and had spent too much time sitting down waiting for them to get right. I also added to his bewilderment by telling him that I did not drive either but walked forty minutes each way to work. He just smiled. I thought that this was the right moment to tell him the hero story. I said it as I had rehearsed it in the waiting room. When I was brave enough to look at his face, Dr Colvin had tears in his eyes and said that it had been nothing.

We went ahead with the official reason for my visit. He examined my legs. I explained my symptoms. There was silence and then Dr Colvin told me that he did not know what to say. The reality was that the operations had been a great cosmetic success, but practically, they were a failure. I don't know how I fought back tears, but I did. The poor doctor continued to tell me that my prognosis was not good. I would need to have orthotics made, wear surgical shoes, and to take pain killers and anti-inflammatory drugs for the rest of my life. He said that he could not understand why I wasn't in continual pain, and said that if the orthotics did not improve things, I would definitely end up in a wheelchair for good, sooner rather than later. He then did the unthinkable for any specialist in any field. My hero apologised. All feelings of self-pity raced out that door, as I assured him that there was no need for that. There had never been any guarantees, and no one had told me that the surgery was a failure and that explained why I had continued to walk when apparently, yet again, I wasn't supposed to.

I asked him what had happened to me in the first place. He explained that it was only now after twenty five years of experience that he could tell me. I had simply inherited all my family's genetic weaknesses in the leg department. My feet had also been formed like a throwback to our tree dwelling days which explained why my feet where flat on the ground with a big toe made apart from the rest of my toes like a thumb. He said that if I had been raised in a shoeless society they would have grown to be hands. That was why I always had to wear boots even to sleep. It was to train my feet to grow properly.

I loved all things scientific, so this fascinated me, once I got over the shock that we were talking about my actual legs, and not the missing link, although that is what it sounded like I was. The consultation came to an end. I thanked him again and we said our tearful goodbyes.

Chapter 15

Separation and the Worst Insult to Planet Earth

I went home in a state of bewilderment. On the one hand I was so happy to meet my hero once more and to thank him, yet I was devastated by the news and at exactly the same time I was almost defiant, thinking that if I'd gotten this far on my feet despite all odds then I'd continue.

As I walked in the door though, only one emotion remained – complete devastation. I lay on my bed and cried, as a tsunami of memories and thoughts picked me up and dropped me.

"So that's why I always hang around with people that other people criticise. It's because I'm a misfit like them. None of us can make it in society.

I am a missing link, no wonder I've never felt as though I fitted in.

My mother was right I can't stand on my own two feet without her help.

I've always been a cripple. I should have known I didn't deserve to have it all work out."

The thoughts were fast and cruel yet somehow at the end of them I was dumped back into a mood of defiance and anger.

"I'm proud to be a part of the misfits. We have a real view of the world with our feet firmly planted on the ground. Not like the stiletto, plastic people who are too scared to do anything for fear of falling on their faces because of their false shaky height."

I liked this thought and decided to end on that note and get on with the life of orthotics and boots. I swore I would not take the medication. After all I wasn't in continual pain. Apparently my body didn't know that it was supposed to be in pain, Medication would be letting it know and, then it might just give me the pain. On a more practical side, if I was on a downhill ride then I'd rather save medication, for when it got really bumpy at the end.

Of course, this new financial burden, added more stress to our marriage that was somewhat crippled itself by now. Orthotics and orthopaedic shoes nearly cost as much as my airfare to New Zealand had. Eventually our arguments got unbearable. Dan wouldn't talk. He was too scared to because I'd probably jump down his throat. I promised to stop arguing, if Dan would stop drinking and partying so much.

We agreed that if we had one more bad year, we should separate until we worked things out. I preferred this to "making it work" as I had grown up with my parents arguing and we wanted more than that for our pride and joy. We did have another bad year and we separated. Tanaya came through seemingly unscathed. She walked at ten months. She knew the alphabet before she was two and she knew how to treat her parents from the day that she was born. She was the perfect child born to some rather faulty parents.

That random thought on the way to my wedding was also now fact. "Nothing lasts forever."

We separated not long before Christmas, as a lot of couples do. We decided not to tell my family until after Christmas, as it would ruin the Christmas spirit if we told them before. We did not hate each other. As a matter of fact we were the best of friends now. There was no reason that we couldn't spend a week together at my parents'.

With everything that had happened in my life I was no longer in tune to anything psychic, or spiritual as a matter of fact I was not in tune at all. This was about to change.

Before we left for my parents I had one of *those* dreams. This time I was at a sand shed party. This was an annual event held at the rutile mine in Redhead. It went from sun down to sun up on Boxing Day. Local bands played. It was invitation only and my sister's friends organised it. I was at the party with Dan dressed in a weird kind of dress. He was with my family and I was alone. Everyone was angry and yelling at me. I woke with *that* feeling but I decided I was safe as there was no chance of us going to that party as we hadn't been to them since Tanaya was born and buying tickets was the last thing we could afford. Anyway I would be yelled at if I went because my mother always reacted that way if I so much as asked her to mind Tanaya over the Christmas family time.

Christmas day arrived and all was going well until Madeline gave a card to both Dan and I. Inside were two tickets for the sand shed party. I looked shocked. Madeline was so pleased to see the surprised look on my face. Madeline had no idea that behind the look was a feeling of sheer horror and dread. I didn't know what to do or say. I talked to mum about my dilemma. She understood *those* dreams as she used to have similar experiences. She reassured me that it would be OK.

These parties were fancy dress. I was going as McEnroe's tennis opponent, complete with blacked out teeth, and tennis racket with strings missing draped over my head. Dan on the other hand could not come up with anything. My sister decided to take care of him while I got Tanaya organised for her night. When I came out, I saw Danny dressed as a caveman. He was wearing mums old fake fur rugs. These formed the weird dress from my dream.

"Ok," I thought, "This dream *is* going to happen. I know how it ends, so I should be able to avoid it."

If only it worked like that. There was nothing that I could do. I hadn't seen the part where the whole catastrophe was started by an innocent dance and Christmas peck on the cheek from an old friend, whom I hadn't seen in a very long time. I could tell you all the family details of who said what and who was hurt the most, but I won't because too many stories like that have been written. Heartbreak is heartbreak.

Months later, the same dear old friend that had caused the whole heartbreaking drama, rescued me from Sydney and took me to a house on a five hundred acre dairy farm in the middle of nowhere in the Hunter Valley. My poor parents went into disownment mode because they were sure I was the one who had done wrong by running off with another man. They didn't know that this other man was up to his ears in his own emotional dramas and certainly wasn't after a lifelong mate, just short term platonic company with a kindred spirit to share the bills while he unravelled himself. He paid for me to take Tanaya to see Danny and to stay there for a week, every six weeks. When we decided that it was time to part, he helped me to move to Newcastle into a small flat.

I began teaching at the local primary school where I had done my first block as a student teacher. One thing led to another and Tanaya and I were offered the chance to move back to my hometown in *the* flat. This flat was even closer to the beach than my parents place in the next block. It was known as *the flat* because in the days when I was busy getting through college, my hometown peers were partying hard in this flat with musicians, the highlight being Cold Chisel. That iconic song, "Cheap Wine and A Three Day Growth" was about parties in *the* flat.

"Sitting on the beach drinking rocket fuel oh… yeah" referred to sitting on Redhead Beach drinking the wild cocktail that our local bartender had made up at *the* flat.

Anyway fate had it that I was able to rent this wonderful party place. I had to take it as I had stuck to my rule of non-pollution of the planet by not owning a car and so I couldn't drive. This meant getting lifts or bussing it for half an hour to work each day. I had to leave Tanaya with my parents on the days that she did not attend preschool. This was also in my hometown.

I wondered how I'd manage moving, as neither Dan nor my dear old friend was around to help this time. Since I'd been teaching in town I had caught up with the remnants of that adopted family from the downstairs' room. One of them was Dale. He was the one that had organised the flat. When I told him my problem, he just told me not to worry. Some of our furniture and belongings had been stored at my parents' house, just around the corner.

He just shrugged his shoulders saying, "You grew up here didn't you? You'll be right."

When I arrived at the flat ready to start the onerous job of moving with the sole help of Dale's wife and her car, I found not only the largest of my possessions at the front door but a line of old and some new friends ready to move them all in. Within an hour my few possessions that had seemed an insurmountable problem in my mind were arranged to make our new home.

My friends left with the sun. Tanaya and I had a quick, first-night meal and I tucked my happy bundle into her bed. I put on a tape of Cindy Lauper's "True Colours" and sobbed until I wailed.

Why? I should have been so happy, but I wasn't. I was right back where I had started. I even had the same leg problem but minus the happy ending. I should have been grateful that I had so many friends, but I had never felt so lonely.

Every one of them was happily enjoying their surf, sun, drugs and rock and roll and that was all we had talked about. That, and how glad I must have been to be back. The fact was I was mortified to be back as I had failed; failed in marriage, failed in standing on my own two feet and definitely failed in my search to find *that* feeling. This and the fact that I couldn't feel grateful or happy caused the wailing. Gratefully, the horrid noise was enough to make me stop in case my daughter woke up thinking a sea creature had invaded her new home.

As the days rolled by I began to feel a little happiness. It couldn't help but grow as I watched Tanaya grow. I was kept very busy in my home town. I hadn't thought that moving home would give me instant employment. As a first year practising teacher, I had left an impression on the local principal who gave me as much casual work as possible. The manager of the bowling club employed me as a poker machine change girl. These two occupations gave me an interesting view of my home town.

I found it difficult to adjust to a sea of blonde headed and blue eyed Aussie kids after the multiculturalism of inner city teaching. It was hard to get used to the fact that I no longer had to spend ninety percent of my time working on behavioural problems. I kept waiting for the war to break out as any calm at my previous schools signalled there was about to be a storm with me in the centre of it. Another odd feature of my classes that I wasn't prepared for was that they nearly all contained the offspring of my old friends' and acquaintances. Some of them looked so much like their parents that I felt as though I had entered a strange kind of time warp. I was also amazed that being a teacher in my home town brought with it a new respect that had certainly been lacking when I was the crippled kid in a surfie culture.

A lot changed in that little flat without me even noticing. I turned my back completely on both my inner world and the friends who had been kindred souls trying to save or at the very least, change the world. I'd started exploring more of the real world and where I fitted in to it, at a rapid pace. I found that I actually fitted into more than one place. I had a popular position in the cool scene; the school scene including parents, teachers and kids; the bowling club circle and with all the oldies who remembered me from when I wore callipers. Even my home was placed at an enviable position closest to the beach. The best part of it all was the fact that I had a beautiful little girl who was popular, clever, happy and unscathed from our divorce. We didn't have any problems with being a broken family because there were so many of them in little Redhead.

One of them was Ruby's family. She had three teenage daughters and a boyfriend who was also everybody's guitar playing guru. She was stunning with a tiny frame, olive skin, a mop of dark long hair and brown eyes that you could swim in. She had been close friends with the girls who had lived in my flat and partied with Cold Chisel and was happy to have her old haunt back again, as well as to have me for a friend. We became close friends quickly which is what cemented my position into the cool scene as she was the epitome of cool. When I wasn't working we spent endless, peaceful days at the beach, visiting friends, drinking coffee or alcohol and talking non-stop. I was never lonely, as our flat was an open house twenty four hours a day whether we wanted it or not. Tanaya was everyone's sweet heart and I was everyone's helping hand.

If by some chance we were alone for too long we just had to walk out our door and there were "the logs" - a gathering place for the entire cool crowd to look at the surf, catch up on gossip by day and by night it was a drinking spot for the "sunset club." Apparently this club had begun in my early days with me as one of the founders! When I asked how this could be so, I was reminded of how sometimes after a night out we would go to the pine log fence at the car park and have one last drink, kiss, swim or whatever one needed to finish a night off, before we went home.

This tradition had changed. Now everyone met there at sunset and discussed plans for the night and returned in the early hours of the morning to continue their night's entertainment. Our small car radios had been replaced by loud pumping music systems and the "one last drink" was replaced by enough to fill a keg. If there were no decent bands playing then the logs became the venue attended by up to fifty people from sunset to sun up. At first I enjoyed this, especially in the summer holidays, as more often than not I would join them. Tanaya would sleep peacefully in her cosy bed, within earshot of us all.

When I felt like escaping I would go and spend time with my parents or visit my sister who lived in Newcastle city itself. My sister and I were still very close. I remember trying to avoid any nightlife other than the logs. The only exception to this rule since becoming a single mother was to go out with Madeline and her boyfriend. That was the only time that mum and dad would agree to baby-sit Tanaya for me. I was happy with that. When I left home Madeline was only fourteen. She was allowed to come and spend time with me during all the stages of my life in Sydney and inherited some of my old friends. She definitely stood on her own two feet in every way right from the beginning. She even played soccer in the first all-girls team and won races in sports events at school. She was a true artist as well and expressed this in everything she did.

When she left school she completed an arts degree in photography and became an art teacher. I was so proud of her, as she was a true individual who was incredibly creative in every way, from her style of clothes which included a long fake fur coat that she had bought in a charity shop the first time she was allowed to go shopping alone, to the cosy clutters of her own art work, shells, pictures, masks and hats that adorned her little terrace in town. Living close to Madeline again had been the only other reason I managed to stop wailing on that first night, so visiting her was something that I always looked forward to. I loved living close to my parents too, but there were times that I felt we were a little too close, given that they could hear all and see all just by walking to the corner. Thankfully, they never did.

Once I became friends with Ruby, things really changed. I had an instant pool of reliable on call babysitters who all loved Tanaya, and I had a close friend, keen to include me in her busy nightlife.

I joined her on weekends. I learnt to go out at the time I would normally have returned and to stay in party mode until sunrise if necessary. My first experience of this scene made me realise that I had never been a part of this scene. I'd looked on but I'd never become involved enough to need a little black dress or anything at all fashionable. This showed on my first night out.

My nights out had been to listen to alternate music that stressed the need for change and we dressed accordingly in charity shop clothes to create a weird mix of punk and pop. Since motherhood mellowed me, my after five wear, changed to a strange mix of hippy and vintage dress. This party scene involved loud original rock and roll music. It involved being fashionable and fitting in. I managed neither on my first night out. Dressed in a long black velvet skirt and a pink heavily sequined cardigan, both from charity shops, I felt as though I was from another era, as I tried to merge into a crowd of tight minis, jeans and cleavage. I avoided being a wall flower as some members of the band were people from my teenage years. Their acknowledgement of me instantly made me accepted. It was as if I had truly returned from another planet. I decided that I had better invest in some more fashionable clothes for this new realm.

That was how *it* happened.

I had committed what I saw in the past as the ultimate insult to planet earth.

I had joined the world of consumerism for fashion's sake. Without even realising it *I* had slipped into that ultimate materialism, the world of fashion.

I even enjoyed watching my transformation and the popularity that came with it. This was not the *I*, I had imagined.

This self-transformation and Tanaya starting school forced me to find a fulltime job, as I now felt the need to have the security of a steady annual income for my materialistic lifestyle. The job I successfully applied for was as a home school liaison officer for a research project looking into the effects on families permanently living in caravan parks. This meant that I had to learn to drive quickly as the area involved was the entire lower Hunter Valley.

Public transport didn't stretch this far so driving was an essential skill which was overlooked in my interview. I had the job but no transport. I had to forget all of my moral objections to driving as it added to the pollution of the planet. The toughest thing I had to forget was my fear of driving itself.

Many of those early dreams that left *that* feeling had involved premonitions of how and where different people I knew were slaughtered in car accidents. I had forgotten all of this with motherhood but getting behind the wheel brought it back in the form of palpitations and perspiration. I told myself that by becoming a driver, I would have control over avoiding any accidents and, as I was so acutely aware of the odds of these occurring, I would do a better job than most. I became the licensed driver of brand new university fleet cars within six weeks of seeing things this way. I loved this job too, as I still loved helping people. I met a myriad of characters in those parks that we all whiz past on our way to somewhere. Tanaya loved school.

Life was fantastic until Ruby invited me to join her in the night scene of rock and roll that existed beyond the logs and the sunset club. Our peaceful days were interrupted by rides on the waves of gossip and inevitable drama that I learnt were a part of this night scene.

"It's just life," Ruby would explain.

I didn't like the dramas whether it was "just life" or not. I couldn't understand why so many adults had to include abusing the love of their lives on their night out, so that all love was inevitably lost by the end the night, and then the entire week was filled with all the "he said and she said" until it was Friday night again and either they made up in time for a repeat performance at a different venue or had the climactic ending on the dance floor. I just didn't get it until I met a man named Adan, who was twelve years younger than me.

With our first kiss I received the unopened script of my own hard to believe drama, and fell ever so blindly into love. Like any well-written drama the beginning was idyllic. When Tanaya was safely tucked into bed, he arrived with flowers and bourbon, and left by declaring his love for me. Tanaya loved him because he spent almost as much time with her as I did. We went everywhere together when I wasn't working, and we even managed a couple of camping trips to secluded beaches.

Eventually he stopped going home, as ours was now his. This was when like so many other failed love stories; the idyllic beginning comes to a sudden end and all those petty little dramas I had never understood in other people's lives entered mine. He got on well with everyone except with my parents.

When I was blinded with love, my parents saw their picture of me torn down in pieces and the crazed face of party-mad, single parent with a toy boy took its place in full colour. We had the worst arguments of our lives because yet again my poor parents were looking through fear and this time it was fear for their only granddaughter. I was looking through the rosiest glasses imaginable. I thought that having a person of colour as a partner was the worst thing that I could have done to the family, but apparently having a blonde haired, blue eyed boyfriend twelve years younger than me was the ultimate in trashing the family heritage.

Now, *we* provided a series of award winning Friday night dramas. The first was the night our paths crossed with my parents' on a night out and we let out an exchange of alcohol fuelled insults with my mother. This was followed by the one when I confronted my new love with the fact that he had been unfaithful with a very young lady. The best dramatic performance was given when he tried to explain the whole situation. Apparently my cool new look had been interpreted as desperate and lonely. This had been the only attraction; a sad lonely single mum on a good income. I was "easy picking".

He followed this with a declaration for sudden undying love. I remember feeling as though I was getting dumped in the surf and when the harsh tumbling of emotion stopped I came up for air with a tirade of "How could you?", "Why would you?" concluding with "I can't ever forgive you."

It was impossible to forgive him because he had not just removed my rose coloured glasses but he had ground them into dust. He had shown me yet another version of how cruel people could be. I provided my poor girlfriend with a week of bad drama by crying and moaning about poor me. The fact that my mother had been one hundred percent correct was what hurt the most.

This might sound unbelievable that a woman in her thirties could be so naive, but when you spend twelve years just getting walking right, you are spared seeing the bad side of people because they figure that you were dealt a hard enough time from birth so you don't need to go through any more.

I couldn't run around as a kid so I was cocooned in a very sheltered life for longer than most. I spent so much time reading girlie books and watching films like Mary Poppins that I had created a world where people were truly beautiful and if they ever were nasty then it was very obvious. My mother had censored all teen magazines which spared me learning about the woes of teenage broken hearts and all that sinful behaviour, as my mother called it.

This young boyfriend sure taught me some very tough lessons about where I was in life. When Dan and I had parted I'd vowed I would never have a partner that was less than him. He had to be better than Dan had been before parenthood took us by surprise.

I recovered from the dramas. The ex-boyfriend left town and I stayed where I was.

Nothing had changed but everything was different.

Chapter 16

The Earthquake and a Gnawing Feeling

Christmas came and we spent it in our traditional way. We had a champagne breakfast; exchanged presents and later drank gin and tonics or dad's great punch, while friends came and went. After lunch, Madeline and I would take to the streets of Redhead to party with friends while Tanaya watched ballroom dancing with her Nar and Par.

The days that followed were spent relaxing. On the morning of 28th December, I remember coming home from a barbecue. Tanaya and I had stayed at Sophie's place because we intended on having more than enough to drink and Tanaya liked to play with Sophie's daughter. We were driving past the beach when *that* feeling that something significant was going to happen, struck. This was the first time that the feeling had come without any dream. It unnerved me. It was so strong.

I almost whispered to Sophie saying, "Today is a …"

I realised I didn't have a clue what to say next, so I just mumbled, "I don't know. It's the sort of day when anything could happen."

Sophie wanted me to explain what kind of thing could happen, but I couldn't so she politely said she knew what I meant.

That day had a truly eerie, ominous dead quiet to it. The ocean reflected this. It was grey and almost motionless. The waves were like a white fringe trimming the edge of the shore and not like waves at all.

When Sophie dropped us at home I began to vacuum and Tanaya watched Romper Room. As I pressed on the vacuum handle I heard a roar like a jet taking off but it was underground. The whole floor began to roll as if it had become a wave. I was convinced that I'd gone mad and Tanaya began screaming as the power was cut and Romper Room's Miss Kim disappeared.

It is amazing how quickly the brain creates thoughts to explain what seems to be inexplicable. From the moment the roar started, my brain had thought of alcoholic poisoning, a leg problem that had somehow affected my brain, or an inaccurate report from the pesticide company that had recently inspected and wiped out the termite mounds that were in our walls, as the cause of this event.

When Tanaya began screaming, "Mummy, what did they do to Miss Kim?" at the top of her voice, my brain switched back to the reality of now and realised that finding a cause was the last thing needed. It told me that now I had to comfort my daughter and at the same time remain calm as the supporting pole in our living room began to shake violently along with everything in the entire house. I was petrified. The floor continued to move in impossible waves. Just as I was clutching Tanaya, convinced that we were about to be swallowed up by the now disused coal mine that must have collapsed, the violent shaking stopped. We were without power but we were still standing.

Tanaya had been given a radio headset for Christmas and it ran off batteries. We shared an ear piece each and listened for news. A news report told us that Newcastle had been hit by an earthquake. The epicentre was in Hamilton; just a short distance from where my precious Madeline lived. A reporter was in Darby Street, the one parallel to my sister's street, describing the destruction. She described the collapse of landmarks and I began to shake violently myself as I raced to the phone. It only rang a couple of times before Madeline answered. She assured me that she was fine and would come out to Redhead as soon as she knew what was happening. Her house had huge cracks in it and the chimney was ready to collapse, so she needed to hang up, as the reality of what she was seeing began to sink in. We didn't know it at the time, but that phone call was meant to be an impossibility because all the phone lines were down.

It was so surreal. *That* feeling had been right again. Something had been about to happen but I could have never imagined this. As that thought took form, I remembered my childhood fears that one day we would have an earthquake but again I was saved from any more thinking, when neighbours that I'd never seen before began knocking on the door. The street had decided that there was sure to be an aftershock, so everyone should gather their valuables and meet at the park in front of our flat near the logs so we wouldn't get crushed by falling debris.

Two things stopped me from carrying out their instructions. The first was the fact that I didn't have a clue as to what I should take, other than Tanaya, and the other was the fact that the park may have been safe from falling buildings but it was at the base of the cliff and there was an electricity cable stretching straight across it. I realised that even being touched by either of these would have meant instant death. I decided to check on my parents who were both OK, as was their home and then take Tanaya to the beach. We waited to see what would happen next. Nothing did.

That night Madeline and her boyfriend came to visit. We sat around the dining room table by candlelight, as the electricity had not been restored. Their day in Newcastle had been a very different one to ours. It was like a war zone. Emergency teams battled to rescue people from the rubble. We looked at each other's faces after we had exhausted ourselves talking about the earthquake. We changed our conversation to how lucky we were and how good it was to sit like this and that it was too long since we had done it. We never imagined that it would take an earthquake to remind us of the simple joy that we had treasured as teenagers. That earthquake put everything into perspective, as all disasters do.

In six seconds it changed so many people's lives forever. It killed thirteen people, injured one hundred and sixty people, damaged sixty thousand buildings and was felt over two hundred thousand square kilometres. It wasn't even a big one, measuring only 5.6. If Australia was the oldest and the most stable continent, I was forever grateful that I was born here and not somewhere like the "shaky isles" as Dan's family had called New Zealand. I couldn't believe that my childhood fear had actually come true, or that I'd had that feeling just before the earthquake struck. I hadn't imagined the eerie stillness. Bushwalkers said that on that morning they didn't hear one sound of nature in the bush or anywhere for that matter. Even the towns yapping dogs were quiet according to those who would know.

I knew the earthquake had stirred memories but I didn't know about the ones just beginning to appear near the surface of the very deep well of time that is buried deep inside all of us.

The entire area of Newcastle literally shook the dirt off, got back up and got on with their lives. Redhead could do it quicker than where my sister lived, as we didn't have to rebuild anything. People had cracks but no visible damage. It was hard to believe that it had ever happened by the time Tanaya went back to school. Life was exactly the same as it had been before the Christmas holidays. It was still an ideal one by most standards but I felt it was missing something and it wasn't a partner, nor was it my beloved grandparents who had passed away. Those things were natural things to happen once you got older, and the pain they cause is recognisable and it passes. It was as if the earthquake had shaken something deep inside of me and forced it to the surface.

This was something so different. This was a gentle gnawing feeling. It was like missing a friend that you hadn't met yet. It came and went like the mysterious rose perfume that came and went in my bedroom. I preferred the scent to the feeling though, as it was comforting, like the smell of my grandparent's Sydney home, but nothing like it. It should have made me paranoid to suddenly have someone's perfume wafting in my bedroom to greet me when I came home, considering I didn't own any of the stuff. Woody Indian oils were the only scents in our home. It was the gentle gnawing feeling that haunted me.

The only thing that stopped it temporarily was my sister leaving for her overseas adventure. She left to teach English in Japan and to travel the world for twelve months. Madeline always talked about it but when she announced that she'd booked her ticket, it was like I'd never heard of her plan. From that moment until Madeline left, we all tried to spend as much time with her as we could.

Tanaya and I couldn't stop crying after she left. It felt the same as when my Nar or Pop died. It was tough, but it stopped, as a sister leaving home was also a natural thing to happen. She wasn't even actually leaving. She was just going on a yearlong holiday.

That gnawing feeling returned and stayed with me every day.

One day not long after this, Ruby and I were walking home from the beach. Out of the blue, she said, "This is the life! We'll be doing this when we're 60, Lisa."

I didn't hear anything else because I was listening to my own voice that had come from nowhere, protesting, "No, we *won't*, or at least *I* won't."

I was as shocked as the expression on her face.

I could tell that I hurt Ruby as she continued, "What more do you want? This is Redhead, man! We've got it all – the best beach and you live in the best spot!"

At the same time that she spoke I felt *that special feeling* – only for a moment, but as strongly as it had been in childhood. It was strong enough to stop the gnawing feeling and to wipe out any thoughts of having hurt Ruby.

I was only being honest.

I continued,

"I know, but one day I'll get a job teaching somewhere, and things will just change." I could already feel that something had changed between us.

It had happened in one moment; in a sentence that came from nowhere.

These words were certainly very heavy with meaning. That moment stayed with me as we walked back to the flat and the gentle gnawing feeling came back. We kept walking. I can still see me turning the key in the lock, as I finally said it, "I know what's wrong. I don't feel *home* anymore."

Ruby's face told me I had to explain.

By the time we were inside drinking coffee Ruby was insisting on an explanation. I could tell her that I just didn't feel right, but I couldn't tell why. I searched but I could not find an answer.

I could tell her all the things that I knew were not the cause. It wasn't because I missed Madeline because this feeling had been around before then. It wasn't the disappointment of my leg prognosis. It wasn't my divorce. It wasn't even any of the possibilities that Ruby came up with. Ruby gave up. I remember walking her to the front door as I prepared to give the answer to poor Ruby, who by now just thought I was being difficult.

"I know it sounds crazy, but do you know what I mean? A true home, a place where…"

I knew Ruby thought this answer was crazy, so I backtracked.

"I love this home and I know this is *it*, but when I was little, home felt more snugly. I felt how I'd feel when I talked to Nar."

Ruby knew all about my beloved Nar. She'd lost her father, so she knew what I meant.

"I want somewhere," a wave of relief came over me as the key to my garbled answer came, "My spirit wants its home. It's like I used to have it and now it's lost. It feels hollow."

Ruby left after another intense but fruitless chat about where on earth this had come from. That night I soul searched and I thought I finally understood. It was because I was missing my spiritual friends. That was it. I had forgotten my ideals. Driving cars, makeup, fashion, gossip, drinking and smoking were never in my plan to save the world and most importantly it was not the way to find that ancient feeling I vowed I would find in my childhood.

Even the logs had become a place of dread for Tanaya and me. In the few years that we had lived here, the sunset club numbers had quadrupled. On some weekends it was a loud, rude presence for the entire forty eight hours. Our flat became more like a public convenience on these weekends. People would call in just to visit the toilet, make a phone call, finish their drink, or borrow a blanket.

Tanaya would ask me to explain the loud conversations from the logs that invaded our home. None of them were fit for a little girl's ears. This all stopped one night when the police were called and arrested around forty people.

It was ironic. We had all been out together that night to listen to my sister's boyfriend's band. We walked home glowing from alcohol as was the dozens of people walking behind us. I went home alone to Tanaya while the others had gone to the logs. Apparently neighbours rang the police as they were finally sick of these party makers. The irony was that this was the first night that I'd slept through the entire ordeal. Paddy wagons arrived and police had fought it out with the sunset club until the wagons were filled. I thought about all this the next night and looked at beautiful Tanaya sleeping peacefully. I decided that we both needed more.

I wrote a poem, as I did whenever something I considered dramatic and self-revealing happened. This one was different. It wasn't stating anything profound like all the rest did. It was simply begging from the bottom of my heart, for my spirit to come home, so that it could show me the way to find more. The poem came from that deep well inside that we all have. It felt as though it was that gentle gnawing feeling talking for the first time. It was begging for comfort.

I put the poem away and forgot it. The gnawing didn't go. It was like a small pin prick hole in a delicately knitted yarn. It went by totally unnoticed until one lot of really hard wear and then it slowly widens until you are forced to notice it and do something about it. Fortunately, I had found it early but I still didn't know how to fix it. I wore it every day and it showed. It affected everything around me. I still loved teaching. No matter how low I thought I felt, everything would change in a moment with something that happened in my classes. With one smile or one sentence from a child, I would get a tingling feeling up my spine that made every hair stand on end. Children were a true joy and I considered it to be a privilege to spend so much time with them.

One day something happened that made me question my sanity again. I had just finished a successful science session filled with tingling moments. I was walking to the staff room savouring the memories when it happened. I began to feel the hair on top of the centre of my head wave around a little bit. It was a weird sensation and it even began to tickle. I stopped and felt for a leaf on top of my head maybe, but there was nothing.

When I went into the stuffy staff room, I put my hand up to where this tickling, gentle movement was occurring to see if there was a strange spider's web attached to my hair making it move. Nothing could have prepared me for what I felt. I could feel a cool breeze very gently coming from the top of my head. It was like a gentle breeze from an air conditioner. I looked up above me to see if somehow I'd missed the fact that we had new ducted air-conditioning or a hole in the ceiling.

There was nothing. I didn't want to tell anyone about this weird inexplicable experience, as I was sure that they would think that I was crazy, especially as now I realised that the breeze was coming from my head and not from up above it. When the others came into the staff room I was jolted from that moment of the incredulous, back to one of staffroom chatter. I joined in and that inexplicable moment slipped from my memory, but the gnawing feeling stayed. At least now I understood that it was my spirit, whatever that was, craving for a home.

The soul searching that came with this realisation led me to see that I needed a class that was mine, if Tanaya and I were to have more. I needed security in my income especially now that my leg problem existed and very shortly I had to replace the very expensive shoes and my very expensive orthotics. So far I was getting away with not wearing them every day. I didn't need the medication that poor Doctor Colvin had prescribed, but I had begun to feel some twinges of pain. If anything happened and my legs decided to believe that they were meant to be in continual pain, I would need a lot more money to pay for it. This in itself should have been enough to make the gnawing feeling but I knew that this had nothing to do with it. Not this on its own.

Getting a permanent teaching job depended completely on a seemingly mythical list that existed in the NSW Department of Education. All names of hopeful employees were given a number and then placed on it. When your number reached the top, you were offered a permanent job in the area that you had chosen. My area was the Hunter Valley. This made the wait longer because this area was very popular amongst teachers that were already employed and wanted transfers. These teachers had priority over those on the list.

I didn't have much time to ponder on the gnawing feeling or the never ending wait for my number to literally come up because my work load had become more demanding. I had quit the research project because I was offered a regular three days a week job at the local school. I relieved every teacher from teaching his or her class for an hour and a half every week. I had to prepare science and art lessons for each class in the school every week.

On top of this, the project that I had worked on, had asked me to put together a kit that would introduce illiterate parents to their child's new school life. This was to be a one hour audio tape and a booklet of illustrated explanations of the necessities for starting kindergarten. Writing the script, recording and editing it were taking more time than I had expected. I spent every spare moment working on it so I would make the deadline I had been given.

Above all of these pressures was precious Tanaya and like every working mother I never felt as though I gave her needs enough time. The amount of time I spent with my cool friends had dwindled down to afternoons at the beach with Tanaya and a few short visits on the weekend. The riot at the logs had quietened things down and caused a lot of rifts in people's friendships. The cool scene was no longer so cool.

Now I only saw Ruby and a few other girlfriends that were close enough to share everything.

Chapter 17

Finding That Feeling

I don't remember when we talked about my gnawing problem or even if I was there when we did. I know that someone said something because one morning after Tanaya left for school, there was a knock on the door and it was Mia. Mia was so cool that she was even too cool for the cool crowd. She was a widower of one of our local surfing heroes who had travelled the world to become a champion.

Since his death she lived in Redhead and raised her son who I'd taught. She was beautiful, and always making the most of life- too busy to hang and chat especially indoors. This was an unusual visit.

We exchanged our usual greetings before she told me why she had come and that she wouldn't stay long. She gave me an advertisement that she thought I would be interested in, from our local paper.

She told me that she knew how I'd been feeling and that this might be the answer. As Mia handed it over she made two statements about me.

"I know you like Indian things."

This was true. I was absolutely fascinated by all things Indian with the exception of its hot food.

"I know you like yoga and meditation."

This was another truth. Before the gnawing feeling had even started, I had paid to do a yoga course with Ruby's eldest daughter and loved every minute of it. When the course finished my teacher told me that I must have been a great yogi in a past life because I was able to easily and perfectly sit in the lotus position. He wanted me to go further with another meditation course. When I told him that I could not afford the fee, his enthusiasm for my future as a yogi changed to that cold hard kind of sympathy that people give when they have the means to help but don't intend to. As his encouragement left, so did my respect for him and his brand of spiritualism.

Yes, Mia was right in her observations.

She continued, "This is a free yoga course and it even has free food and music included."

It sounded like a possible answer. It took one moment for me to decide to go and to offer to be the driver for us, as I assumed that Mia was looking for a yoga buddy.

"No! No! It's not my thing but I just knew how you'd been feeling; saw the ad and thought of you."

That was one of those special moments that are invisible to everyone except the person whose heart is being affected by it. It was special because in that flash I remembered all the time that I had spent looking up from my wheelchair at all the cool people; the time that I had spent running from what I'd labelled the mentality that they all suffered from, and at the end of it I realised that I was standing on my own two feet as an adult at home looking at one of the coolest people in the eye and they were here to help me. Those cool people had become my friends. Their mentality seemed Ok too.

That moment showed me that moving home had moved me. It moved me from the position of a crippled child, still sitting in the wheelchair from her childhood to one of an adult standing on her own two feet. Here I was.

Mia saw all of this flicker across my face and just said, "Whad'ya reckon?"

I was grinning when I agreed and I grinned even more when I finally saw the ad. There was a photo of a woman whose face was so round and happy that it just made you smile. There it was in black and white- a free four week course for two hours a week that included live Indian music and refreshments. It was to be held Saturdays at 1.00pm, in Charlestown Library. The library was near my old primary school, so I knew exactly where it was even though I'd never been into it in my life. This was reassuring as at this stage I was still a very nervous driver. Driving still felt like a life threatening activity to me that I never managed to enjoy. If I had to go to an unfamiliar destination I would always drip in embarrassing perspiration by the time I got there and that was even when I had a navigator by my side. I was a pathetic driver so this familiar venue knocked down this barrier preventing me from reaching there solo.

The time and day were perfect for getting my parents to baby-sit. Sunday was lawn bowls day but Saturdays they were at home. They would be more than happy to mind Tanaya for the four weeks if I was doing something more constructive than drinking alcohol, chain smoking, and dancing to loud music.

Mia was an angel. A lot had changed when I got that little ad. It felt like this was the long awaited cure for my gnawing feeling whatever it was. Mia left feeling happy that her visit was successful.

I had a full week to wait for the course to begin. It only took that long for the idea of going to it, to fall from a being an essential cure for my problem to being a just another thing to do before the dreaded deadline. This deadline was looming in the week after the course began. By this time my brain had long forgotten how to play the game of making words become meaningless sounds. Words were now a part of every moment of existence, because I never stopped thinking. Even when I was asleep my brain busily worked on creating the complete perfect class program, the lesson for a difficult child, drawings for booklets or a crochet pattern for a jumper for Tanaya, and that was on top of all the normal sorting out of the day's events and problems that our mind does when we are asleep. I'd always wake up exhausted.

This week my brain was working overtime. I'd spent so much time thinking that I'd hardly gotten anything done at all, let alone the manuscript. Time had almost run out and as usual I'd left the work until the last minute. My busy mind worked hard to convince me that I couldn't go to the course after all.

I had to miss it if I was going to save my professional credibility by handing in my kit on the deadline that the university had set.

I was only being sensible and responsible, my brain assured me.

It was crazy to create more stress by expecting my poor brain to begin to learn something new in the middle of giving birth to a work of genius that would solve all the misunderstandings between parents and schools.

I just couldn't go. At this point in my life I was just too busy.

I remember all these thoughts running through my mind as I was drifting to sleep a couple of nights before the course began.

None of this was worth remembering.

It was what happened the next morning that made it all memorable. I woke up and sat straight up without a sliver of sleep left.

It was there. It was the strongest it had ever been.

It was *that* feeling; the one that came when last night's dream meant the future. This time though it didn't involve anything ominous or fatal.

I let the dream wash back over me and watched it as though I was sitting back in a cinema watching it on a huge technicolour screen. It began with me in a library, searching for books, collecting them and carrying piles of them into another room. I did this three times and each time I passed the doorway to a bigger room. Every time I walked passed that doorway I looked into the room over the pile of books and saw people getting ready for something. On the wall opposite the doorway that I looked through, was a painting of a serene woman with long hair lying asleep on her back in a small boat on a beautiful river in a forest. I had no knowledge in reality that this painting existed. It was a print of the "Lady of Charlotte" by John Atkinson Grimshaw.

On my last trip with my pile of books, I actually stopped in the doorway. I saw two men. One of them had blonde hair and the bluest eyes and the other had darker hair with a twinkle in his eyes that made it difficult to see their colour. They were sitting on the ground getting ready to play music. The blue eyed man had a guitar and the twinkling eyed one was sitting in front of an Indian keyboard instrument. I couldn't remember its name but I knew that it was Indian and that these men must have been the musicians for the yoga program. As I stood there making these connections they were observing me.

They got up and walked to the doorway I was standing in.

The one with the blue eyes said to me, 'What a shame you *think* that you are so busy?"

"This is just for you. This is *just* what you need." said the other.

"Yeah," agreed the blue eyed man with a wide smile, "Because you *think* you are so busy, you'll miss out and it'll only be because you *think* that you are so busy."

"It's all up to you," continued the twinkling eyed one.

At this point I could feel myself juggling the books because of the surprise that these words gave me. Before these men could say anything else I had chosen to end the dream.

I woke up and with the last wisp of that memory of the dream, came a strong blast of *that* feeling. I had almost forgotten this feeling. The best part of it this time was that it involved a positive event and nothing fatal or heartbreaking. This time that feeling was fantastic and it was telling me to go to that program no matter what.

The day for the first lesson in this yoga came. I wore bright blue knitted pants with big coral pink butterflies outlined in black and a matching top. I thought this would be appropriate to manage any strange postures and I always wore it on grey rainy days because it cheered them up. It was a grey rainy day when I set off to that program. Mum and Dad had agreed to mind Tanaya each week, so there was nothing to stop me now. I drove to the library alone, almost chain smoking my Benson and Hedges Virginian cigarettes with a nicotine content of sixteen. I felt a little nervous even though I knew where I was driving because it had been a long time since I had done anything, let alone a course without a friend or colleague being with me. This was very different.

I arrived early because as always, I had factored in time taken for possible traffic jams, car breakdowns, traffic light failure and whatever other catastrophe that could occur on route so as never to be late for any significant appointment such as catching a train, a doctor's appointment, a job interview or in this case the first day of a course.

I sat outside the library and lit up my very last cigarette. There were a few other people outside but not a crowd which was a relief to me. I had the last puff of my cigarette as they opened the doors for us to enter. I bent down and stubbed it out on the rocks of the bush garden surrounding the entrance to the library. I kept my eyes on the ground as I followed the group into the room where our course was awaiting us. I looked up only to pick a seat. I hoped it would be close to the back of the group, but unfortunately I was forced to take a seat close to the front and in the middle of the group.

When I finally got seated and comfortable, I looked around me. I smiled as I saw the painting from my dream hanging exactly where I had seen it, and two men were sitting on the floor just as they had been in my dream. They *were* the men from the dream!

To the side and slightly in front of them in the centre of the group was a very small television and video on a trolley, just like the ones we used in the school libraries. Standing to our right and beside the screen was a young man with dark hair and eyes framed by glasses. He was conservatively dressed, not at all like the yogis I'd imagined. As a matter of fact no body was dressed as I had imagined except for an Indian lady who wore the traditional Indian loose fitting cotton pants and matching long top, called a salwar kameez.

The men wore either jeans or conservative trousers. Most women wore jeans or loose fitting pants and a tee-shirt or blouse of some kind. Some women however wore long skirts with blouses and cardigans as though they had stepped out of a European fairy story. They seemed to glow. Some of these women wore long necklaces of two strands of black beads that were not strung but joined by golden or silver metal links. These necklaces intrigued me and I studied the beads resting on the back of the woman's neck sitting in front of me and just to the right.

When we were all seated the man introduced himself, and welcomed us, before proceeding to nervously describe the order of events. He spoke with a slight lisp.

The talk didn't last for long and my brain began racing with critical thoughts from the moment it began,

"How could he teach us about yoga? He's too nervous and doesn't even sound or look like a calm person. I've made a big mistake coming."

He told us that we would feel vibrations when a mothering energy that we all had was awakened and that we would feel a cool breeze coming from the top of our head.

"This is crazy talk! As if that could happen! I have to go," my mind screamed at me. I didn't even remember the strange breeze on my head that day at school.

As he got to the point where he told us that we would be looking at a video of a talk by the founder of Sahaja yoga, Shri Mataji Nirmala Devi who would explain this process called self-realisation that would spontaneously establish our connection to this energy, my mind told me to get up and leave because now this group was guilty of false advertising. That beautiful lady was not going to be there in person, the way that the ad had let me believe. My brain concluded that it looked boring and sounded crazy.

The thoughts finished as his talk finished. I was ready to walk out when the lights went out on cue, and the play button was hit and the video began. In the same moment I pictured the group's disapproval if I stood to leave blocking the small screen that by now all eyes were glued to. I couldn't leave. I'd missed the chance. I had to stay put as I couldn't face the picture I'd conjured up of everyone snarling at me to tell me to sit down, becoming a reality.

I tried to relax and just listen. This woman's talk made this happen as everything that she said seemed to make the most sense I had ever heard. She seemed to be answering questions that I had forgotten even asking. She had the missing piece to the jigsaw of my life at that moment. It was like she was the kind stranger that finds a lost child and comforts them by explaining how they will help them to get back home safely. She made me feel that cosy warmth and comfort of my mum's chenille clad arms.

She talked about the stresses in our lives and how we are all searching for something and that this something is truth.

She explained that it is our spirit that wants us to know our true self and what our purpose is in this life. This is what we are all really searching for. I realised that this searching had caused my gnawing feeling.

She talked about the world problems and how they were created by humans and leading us to disaster. She talked about the stress that all these problems cause us in our lives because we are always worrying about the past or present and what we have to do.

She stressed the need to change.

She reminded us that all anyone has is the present. The past and the future don't exist. If we could stay in the present then we would be able to enjoy our lives. The way to do this, she explained was to slow down or stop our thoughts, as it is impossible to think about the present.

I loved what she said as it reminded me of how I'd played my game of trying not to even let the meaning of words enter my brain so that I could escape the weight of their meaning. She was talking about the inner world that I had spent so much time in during my childhood. It had been my saviour in my childhood and now I was being reminded of it for the first time in decades. She was even explaining it. These were the explanations that I had wanted but had been too young to even think to ask for. I felt so comforted by every word that this woman was saying.

She talked about collective consciousness which I vividly remembered getting a short mention in a lecture on Yung at college. She told us that the name of obtaining this true knowledge about ourselves was called self-realisation, another term I vividly recalled from the same lecture. She explained that this is what human beings needed to obtain in order for our lives to change. This change was needed to save our planet from what could be destruction caused by all the problems that we had created such as global warming, pollution and the wars we fight daily, both globally and internally.

My mind was being washed with the most soothing words that I had heard since I was a child. I wasn't crazy, I was actually right and I wasn't the only one that had a gnawing feeling hidden under our comfortable fashions.

She began to explain how we would obtain our self-realisation, the key to this yoga. I now understood that Sahaja Yoga was not going to be exercises but rather the true meaning of the word which is union with the divine or that cosmic consciousness that so many referred to. Of course I loved this idea but by now I had reached the point of absolute disbelief in anyone trying to claim that they were in touch with anything higher than their own brain.

She was different though. She was still talking the talk that I had craved for as a teenager. Shri Mataji told us that the word "Sahaja" meant spontaneous or born within and this meditation was called that because we are all born with a special energy inside of us that would be spontaneously awakened as soon as we asked for this to happen. Once this energy awakened, we would have our self-realisation and a new awareness called thoughtless awareness that we would maintain through meditation. She explained how we would achieve this.

I don't remember whether it was Chris or Shri Mataji that explained that this was why Sahaja yoga was always free. We already possessed this mothering energy that was lying dormant in all of us, so we couldn't be made pay for what we already had. All Sahaja yoga would do is to teach us how to use it. I was especially impressed with this part. Despite the conservative appearance of this group, they were not chasing the dollar like so many gurus were.

As I was finishing that thought, Shri Mataji continued with the most brazen statement that I had ever heard anyone spiritual say.

It was simply this, "Keep an open mind like a scientist, and see for yourself that what I tell you is true."

She told us just to try it and we would experience the benefits. It was not a matter of believing in anything to be the truth. It was simply a case of experiencing it. At the same time as my brain was telling me perhaps this beautiful woman was a little crazy, I felt like cheering my heart out at the sound of those words. Luckily for me on both counts her soothing words kept flowing and I was washed away with them. I was heading back to my inner world and this lady was taking me to it along a path that I'd never known.

Shri Mataji told us to treat what she told us as an experiment and to do the techniques daily and that after a month we would have experienced it and know it as the truth. She said it was like electricity when it was discovered. You could explain all the wonderful things that it would do and how it works, but until we turn on a switch to use it or plug something into it, it is impossible to really understand how fantastic it is. Once the light switch is on, there is no doubt that electricity is a powerful invisible force that lets us see into the darkest of places. Once we experience it we don't believe in electricity we know it is real. The fact that it exists is the truth. This was what this energy we all had was like. These aren't Shri Mataji's exact words but that was her message.

She went on to explain what we were to do in order to experience this new dimension of Sahaja Yoga and so begin our experiment with truth. She explained once more that because of the state of the world we live in, we always exist in the past or future but rarely do we exist in the present. We are forever worrying or at least thinking about the past or the future. When we do this we put pressure on not just ourselves but on energy centres within us called chakras and we cause these centres to become imbalanced, just like ourselves sometimes!

We learnt that these centres correspond to the major plexuses of the body. It is the energy of these centres that look after our internal organs. What we don't understand is that these centres are also where other qualities like forgiveness, creativity, satisfaction, diplomacy, collectiveness, discrimination to name but a few, lie. When we lack in these qualities or go to extremes in expressing them, the centres become imbalanced.

Shri Mataji explained that we have this very subtle system inside all of us, that was made up of not just the chakras but also three channels that represent the past, future and present. The central channel was the present; the one to the left was our past as well as all our emotions and conditionings associated with it; and to the right was our future, including all of our creativity, planning and actions associated with it. She said that all this was ancient knowledge, and at the base of our spine inside our sacrum bone laid a three coiled dormant energy that was like our spiritual mother just waiting for us to ask her to wake up and give us the truth about ourselves in the most loving way. This is the reason that the ancient Greeks had called this triangular bone sacrum meaning sacred.

She said that when we asked for this energy to be awakened it would uncoil and begin to move upwards along the back of our spinal cord, gently trying to clear out any tensions and to bring all our chakras or plexuses into balance. When it reached the top of our head it would pierce the fontanel bone and we would feel it as a gentle cool breeze. Some of us would feel it as heat because that is how the negative energies that we may have accumulated would feel as they left our bodies. The word fontanel was quoted as more proof that this is ancient knowledge, as the word meant fountain and this is how this energy felt when it was able to move unhindered straight to this area to give us our yoga, our union with this energy. Some people might call this energy Divine and others may just call it that energy that is in the cells of every living thing around us.

It was explained that when stresses build up too much pressure for our poor old bodies to bear, we get sick. With self-realisation we would have access to inside knowledge about our very being. We would also experience our thoughts being soothed away until we experienced thoughtless awareness, as then we would be in the present where thoughts don't exist. This mothering energy would free us from all this and bring us into the present to experience thoughtless awareness.

In this state she told us that we would also begin to feel sensations on our fingers. Each finger was now a part of this incredible system she was describing, as each one corresponded with a chakra. If a finger prickled or felt hot, it meant that the corresponding chakra was out of balance. Shri Mataji said that this way we would know our true inner selves. We would also learn to fix these imbalances so we could avoid sickness as disease is just that- lack of ease in our bodies.

Shri Mataji described this energy as being like a rope with many strands and our chakras were like beads lying in its path waiting for the energy to pass through them and bring them into one straight string of pearls. If our chakras were too far out of alignment then only a few strands would make it through to pierce our fontanel bone, because the rest would be blocked in each bead so it would be only a "small, small breeze" as she so sweetly put it.

She was truly the most fascinating person but when she kept talking about the cool breeze business, I just couldn't believe it. I stayed anyway and listened to every word because the minute my brain came up with a raging criticism, she would soothe it with the sweetest words, and besides that I'd already missed my moment of escape.

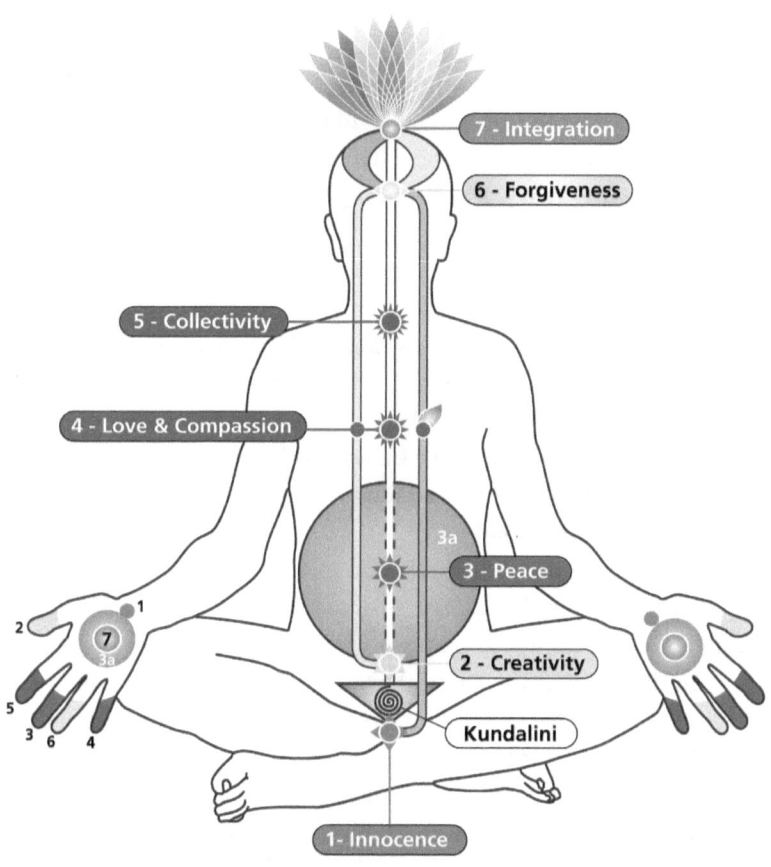

The Subtle System

Chapter 18

A Small Breeze and the Comforter

The time had come when we were to take off our shoes, sit comfortably on our chairs and follow her directions as she led us on our journey to self-realisation. She had shown us the positions we were to place our hands. She had explained that we would use our right hand to do them as it represented our right side especially our actions, and we would place our hand on the left side of our body, as it represented our desire or our left channel. By doing it this way, we were showing that we truly desired this energy to awaken and give us our self-realisation.

Our left hand would rest, palm turned upwards on our lap, again representing our desire for this to happen. We would have to begin by asking this energy to awaken and then we were to silently say affirmations at each chakra. The number of times that we repeated the affirmations would correspond to the number of petals that each chakra had. I couldn't believe it! Here was an explanation to the flowers I had adored watching as I went to different levels of my inner garden as a child.

My brain didn't have a chance to think about this revelation as she continued with our last instruction which was to call our energy, "Mother" as it was our spiritual nurturer.

In the front of the room there was a small, simple table with a picture of Shri Mataji on it. In front of the photo was a burning candle. Next to the table was that small television with its built-in video player. The screen on which the same lady's face appeared was tiny but truly, to this day I will say that it was as though she was there in larger than life form. I even felt as though I had met her before and somehow lost contact. I was putty in her hands even though I thought that what she was saying would happen was crazy. I was hanging on her every word but I was sceptical. I was certainly in the mindset of a scientist as she instructed us to close our eyes to complete the technique we were all here to learn.

This is how the technique was explained in her calm voice that came from that little screen. The words may not be exact.

Shri Mataji

"We will work on the left hand's side with the left hand pointed towards me. Now first of all you can ask this three times. All put your hand on your heart. Here resides your spirit and here we ask 'Am I the spirit?'"

We used the term "Mother" to refer to the mothering energy or kundalini because it was like our mother in that it knew all about us and was a loving energy.

Shri Mataji continued, "Now put your hand on your left upper stomach-just below the ribs and ask, 'Am I my own guru?' or you can say, 'Am I my own master or teacher?'

Again ask the question three times. Move your hand down to the lower portion of your abdomen – just below the hip and with some pressure on it. Here we ask six times, 'Mother, please give me true knowledge.' You must ask for it as it cannot be forced on you. This energy will only awaken if *you* desire it. You can call it mother. Say, 'Mother pleases give me the true knowledge?'

Now raise the right hand back to the upper abdomen and say, 'Mother, I am my own master.' Say this ten times. The actual number doesn't matter so much but you must say it from your heart

Now place the hand on your heart and say, 'Mother, I *am* the spirit?' You are not all your troubling emotions but you are the spirit.

Next turn your head to the right and place your hand on the place where the shoulder meets the neck and say, sixteen times 'I am *not guilty.*' To make mistakes is to be human and we should not feel guilty. Don't worry how many times you say it, just mean it.

Now put your hand across your forehead and let the head rest on it a little bit and say, 'Mother I forgive everyone for everything.' Don't think about this now. Just forgive in general and forgive yourself also. Say 'Mother I forgive everyone for everything' and say it as many times as you want but say it from your heart.

Next place your hand now on the back of your head and tilt your head backwards onto your hand and say, 'Please forgive me, if I have made any mistakes.'

Now place your palm on the top of your head where I showed you and stretch your fingers back, applying pressure and rotate the hand slowly clockwise —so that the scalp moves a little and say, 'Mother please give me my self-realisation.' Say this seven times.

Now raise your hand above the fontanel area and see if you can feel a little breeze. It may be cool or it may be a little bit hot —doesn't matter. Alright now slowly open your eyes. All those that have felt this cool breeze all raise both your hands and let's see."

Chris stood and turned off the tape, as almost every person including myself raised their hands in the air. He told us to lower our hands and to sit as we had in the beginning and to just look at the photo of Shri Mataji. If we began thinking we were told to watch our thoughts like a movie rather than getting involved with them. This was my first meditation although I didn't know it at the time. All I knew was that my busy brain had finally stopped for the first time since college and I was beginning to feel the strangest sensations in my hands. It felt a little like the feeling you get after having pins and needles when you feel the blood rushing back to the effected part. Some of my fingers felt as if they were being pricked with needles.

Chris asked what we had felt. All of us could say something. Chris explained that these sensations were this mothering energy beginning to clear out all the imbalances that we had accumulated over our hectic lives and that now we were going to clear these imbalances a little more with the help of other yogis that were present. I later learnt that in Sahaja yoga, a yogi was simply a person who had their self-realisation and had established their connection to this mothering energy. The "glowing people" that I had noticed at the beginning of the program were the yogis.

My yogi was a beautiful lady called Stephanie, with silver hair to her shoulders pulled back in a ponytail. She sat behind me and quietly told me to look at the photo, as a focal point and to keep my attention on top of my head ignoring my thoughts as they came. I knew that I wouldn't be touched so this made it easier to relax. I felt tiny puffs of air around me as this total stranger whirled and flicked her hands behind me. I could actually feel the sensations in my fingers change and some of the prickling stop. In its place was an amazing coolness and complete relaxation of my being.

When Stephanie finished, she asked if I was Ok. What a question! Ok didn't even come into it as I was now experiencing an entirely different state of being where "OK" didn't even seem to exist. I managed a nod and almost resented Stephanie's kind intrusion into my first encounter with this truly mothering energy.

Chris introduced the musicians from my dream, who had played briefly before the beginning of the program. They played Indian music that was ancient and yet familiar. Once again I got the comforting feeling that I had not felt since my mother's chenille clad arms wrapped around me as a child and it made me feel inspired somehow.

When they finished we were asked to comment on the music. The older women in the front row jumped to speak, telling us about wonderful journeys and a feeling of returning home. Others spoke of memories of their own mothers and one woman even cried as she recalled her emotional unveiling that the music had caused. I couldn't think of anything to say because the music made me thoughtless!

The last part of the formal program was a demonstration of how to meditate at home, receiving handouts and an invitation to stay for refreshments. I haven't got a clue as to what I ate or what I said but I do know that the food I ate tasted as though I was tasting for the first time and the people I met that were practising Sahaja yoga were like nobody I had ever met before, yet I felt like they were my long lost friends.

One couple stood out: the woman because of her glowing beauty and the man because of his dark shining eyes. This couple introduced themselves as Lene and Guy. They were married. Lene was wearing one of those intriguing necklaces. When I commented on it she explained that it was a symbol of their marriage, just like a wedding ring is.

I remember meeting the musicians from my dream. They were introduced as John and Kevin.

That is all I can recall of our conversation. I just remember feeling wonderful. The gnawing feeling had stopped and the best part was that my brain was calm. I didn't leave chanting mantras or jumping for joy. I just left smiling and I even enjoyed the drive home.

I didn't realise anything beneficial had happened at all when I stopped off at the corner shop and stood there having totally forgotten what I needed to buy. I thought I had all the necessities at home, but bought milk and bread anyway.

On my way out I was stopped by a girlfriend that I used to smoke pot with, who exclaimed, "Whatever you've had, I want some! Your eyes look amazing."

I was completely taken aback. I muttered where I had been and that maybe this was the cause of my eyes apparent beauty.

I didn't realise that something quite significant had taken place that day until later that night when I reached for my cigarettes and realised for the first time that I hadn't smoked since before the program and that in fact this had been the sole reason for my visit to the shop- to buy my essential packet of twenty five sixteen milligram nicotine cigarettes, that I had consumed daily for eight years. I remembered Gibbo's comment. It seemed that this meditation was the thing that would take smoking's place.

I knew something incredible had happened when days past and I was still feeling like a non-smoker. It was as if smoking had given up on me instead of me giving it up. I did the ten minutes meditation and when thoughts came I would say, "Not this thought" and just watch it like a film. Watching thoughts and not getting involved with them was called witnessing. We were told to try and stay thoughtless throughout the day and just say, "Not this thought" as we did in meditation. I have to admit that sometimes I would be babbling "not this thought" as my busy brain would just take off as it was so used to doing and some days it would win.

Over the next four weeks we learnt a little more about deciphering our vibrations, as these new sensations were called. We learnt how to raise our mothering energy and how to protect ourselves from life's daily stresses. We learnt to understand what different vibrations meant in terms of imbalances within and how to correct them with simple techniques using only bowls of salty water to soak our feet in or a couple of simple household candles. We watched more videos of Shri Mataji's talks and every one of them seemed to be answering so many doubts and questions that I had given up on ever finding answers to. Somewhere in my mind was a growing niggling feeling that I had seen her before that first program. I never paid much attention to this feeling as I was too involved with learning about this simple meditation. It wouldn't matter how many stresses I felt before I went to a program, they would all dissolve by the time I left.

I learnt that my hot prickling thumbs meant that I was thinking and planning too much. It wasn't surprising to me that after a week of foot soaking my right thumb actually broke out in blisters. I obviously had the greatest imbalance as I was the only one that had this dramatic result. I was just relieved that they didn't self-combust when I thought back on how even in sleep my thoughts kept planning the future or literally jumping into it to have those unpleasant premonitions. I was so glad that all this was now a thing of the past.

I learnt that my prickling little left finger meant that I needed to take long slow breaths while saying "I am the spirit" until it eased. I was grateful that I only felt these sensations when I was meditating as life with fulltime prickles and heat would be a little uncomfortable. Unlike other activities involving health in my past, the beneficial qualities of Sahaja Yoga were instant, stronger and longer lasting than the negative ones.

I had begun to understand the term "self-realisation." It was simple. It meant just that – beginning to realise who I really was. I was learning some important truths about me. I learnt that the whole gnawing feeling episode was my spirit trying to tell me that it had to be recognised and allowed to express itself.

I could see I had not been happy for years, the unhappiest time being when I learnt that my legs no longer had the fairy tale ending attached to them. When that happened I had given up completely on the notion of God or anything spiritual. After all it seemed a very cruel joke to find out that after enjoying a decade of normal life standing on your own two feet, I now had to wear bulky orthotics and daggy shoes just to stop falling over and that my retirement plan, if I ever made one, now had to include a house with no steps and a wheelchair. I might even have to change this retirement plan into a lifestyle change years before my retirement age. That on top of a failed marriage had stripped me of any remaining spirituality and desire to help save the world. Yet all of this was wiped away by this mysterious lady, Shri Mataji.

When I moved back to my home town, I had simply become a chameleon, to fit in with other people. I became the cool nightclubbing single when I was with my sister's friends; the radical "let's live for the moment" person when I was out with the cool scene; the modern primary schoolteacher at work and finally a mum that kept her opinions quiet so that her daughter and her were accepted by the right circles. I was good at being all these characters. I had transformed from one to the other without ever noticing. I had inherited a new me. At the time I truly thought it was all the real me and I didn't even know that I was unhappy with it all. Tanaya had been the only good thing in that whole time.

When I moved into that flat I had moved out of myself. No wonder I balled my eyes out on that first night. I saw all this about myself as I gradually moved back into my true self.

I began to see Sahaja Yoga changing my life. For the first time since I was a child I was actually enjoying getting out of bed early no matter what the day had in store for me. I completed my project effortlessly and on time. It impressed my supervisor and she even wanted my voice on the final recording. Normally I would have become a nervous wreck at the thought of learning to use studio equipment and recording my voice. This was the voice that was described by one lecturer as "boring and monotone and a hindrance to being a teacher." Instead I couldn't wait to learn a new skill. I enjoyed every minute in the recording studio, even the embarrassing ones riddled with mistakes.

I was enjoying both food and cooking for the first time since I had moved to the flat.

Every night I hopped first into a foot soaking dish, then into meditation for ten minutes. My bedtime had gradually gotten earlier and every night I felt like I was cocooned in that chenille dressing gown and had peaceful sleeps free of any more disturbing dreams that brought that feeling of dread.

I had decided from the first experience that I liked this self-realisation. I was like a shrivelled up sponge that wanted to soak up every drop of information about this phenomena that was causing so many practical changes in me. I didn't go out and read books about Sahaja Yoga because back then, there were few available and just as well because I didn't have time to read them anyway.

As the weeks rolled on, I learnt all about myself and still nothing much about this process. That was the best part of it all. You simply had to do easy enjoyable things that only took up twenty minutes a day and there was absolutely no reading or learning or practising involved. You simply had to experience these subtle effects and they led you to whatever knowledge *you* needed.

After our last program, Lene and Guy asked how I had enjoyed the course and the meditation. I told them that it was the best thing that had happened to me and that I was sad that it had come to an end. Lene asked if I used a photo and a candle when I meditated. I told her that I just used a candle and the black and white leaflet that we had been given at our first program. I admitted that I had only managed to meditate in the evenings as I thought mornings would be impossible as there wasn't enough time. I smiled as I said that because I realised I hadn't even tried to do it even though I got up earlier. I had just thought about it.

A few days later a beautiful photo of Shri Mataji arrived in the post along with an invitation from Lene and Guy to spend a weekend at their home in Sydney. I left the letter and photo on the table and it was still there when I brought Tanaya home from school.

As soon as she entered that room she went straight to the photograph and exclaimed,

"Wow mum! Who's this lady? I bet she is really spiritual."

She may as well have told me that she could understand Greek. I would not have been any more stunned. Here was a six year old child, who had never seen an Indian woman wearing a red dot on her forehead and a sari before, and had never talked to me about anything at all spiritual as I had turned my back completely on religion since my marriage, telling me that this strange photo in her home was of a very spiritual person. That thought truly hadn't even entered my mind. I saw Shri Mataji as a person with wonderful knowledge of our evolution and of society's problems. Her advice was so practical and down to Earth that I hadn't even stopped for a second to see it as anything spiritual. I cautiously agreed and told Tanaya all about this lady and the meditation. She was very impressed and then she went on to watch her beloved Playschool.

Tanaya's reaction and the thought of meditating with Lene and Guy when we visited made me vow to make morning meditation a part of my daily routine. Once again I was stunned as I managed to do it effortlessly, and I even began to be a real morning person. Tanaya joined in with me when she woke up in time.

At that last program I received a second invitation to attend nightly programs with other people who lived in Newcastle and practised Sahaja meditation. Tanaya had been included in the invitation as this meditation was meant for families and not all about indulging the individual as the other one that I had tried had been. Tanaya's reaction to the photograph and her short meditations assured me that she would be a keen participant. At first my parents minded her so that I could learn more without being distracted. I also needed to know for a fact that the change of venue didn't mean any hidden weirdness.

The only thing that was different *was* the change of venue. The rest was just as rejuvenating and intriguing as all other programs. If anything it was better as there were no time restraints in Chris's home. In those first weeks, I was always the last person to leave as Chris patiently answered every question in great detail.

Finally, Chris gave me a booklet about Sahaja yoga so that I had my answers in writing. It was a beginner's book that set out everything that I had already learnt in more detail. It gave all the Sanskrit names of the chakras and explained more about their qualities. It also presented the concept that on each of these chakras resided a deity. I didn't really understand what a deity was, as Catholicism certainly didn't ever mention deities other than in the singular form when referring to their God.

I read the book completely the night after I received it. Although it talked of things that totally contradicted almost everything that the church taught, it did include some of the things that, of all people, my Nar had talked to me about in our long conversations about God and saving the world. I felt like I finally had the key to the truth about God whatever that meant.

It explained vibrations as being an awareness that occurred when that mothering energy united our individual consciousness to the universal, and we were suddenly tuned in to the universal wavelength of vibrations. These vibrations pervade the cosmos but before realisation, we know nothing about them, except maybe whispers of them when we act on a gut feeling and it turns out to be the truth. When our mothering energy breaks the shell, we can experience these vibrations as a part of our daily lives. They were the universal truth if you like. What was more incredible was that if you asked these vibrations questions then we would be given answers. A cool breeze would mean a positive response and warm sensations were the negative answer. Chris had told us about this and we even tried it out. When we were in meditation it never failed. At home I even tried it out under my blankets, just to be sure that the coolness was really coming from my palms.

The last part of that book blew my mind. It wasn't what it said but what it asked and the answer that came to me.

It read like this,*"............through the vibrations that radiate from her, your kundalini is awakened, you feel those vibrations. Because of her you can awaken kundalini; you can give realisation, you can cure sickness; you can share this message of divine love with the whole world. There must be a reason and there must be a meaning. Ask yourself the question .Who is Shri Mataji Nirmala Devi?"[1]

I sat on my bed cross legged and began to meditate without any ritual of candle or photo and I asked myself that question. I felt an amazing coolness and a flood of thoughts that fell into place. These were those thoughts,

"God had always said he would send a comforter.

He said that he would send the Holy Spirit.

Shri Mataji must be that comforter.

She is the incarnation of the Holy Spirit.

We are all made in God's reflection.

There is the Father, Son and Holy Spirit. If we are made in His reflection then there must a female aspect of God. That must be the Holy Spirit. The Holy Spirit must be the Mother and that must be Mary.

Shri Mataji was the Holy Spirit. She was Mary.

---

[1] pg. 56-57 "Sahaja Yoga" publishers Nirmala Yoga-43 Bangalow Rd, Delhi 110007 (India)

Another flood of inspiration and cool vibrations told me that somehow she was the embodiment of all religions and that if I had been of another religion or culture, I would have received the answer Rainbow Serpent, Great Spirit, Ruoch Hakadesh, Ruh, Chi, Tao, pure universal love, cosmic energy or whatever word was used in that culture or religion for the divine energy that is beyond human understanding.

If this scene had been a part of a movie, there would be streams of heavenly light and angels singing or some heavenly, "Hallelujahs." But this was no movie, this was my life: this was me in my room alone experiencing a reality. I slowly opened my eyes and untangled my legs to walk around to be sure I was truly still functioning normally and had not suffered some kind of physical and mental episode. After all, it isn't every day that knowledge like this just arrives in your mind with absolute clarity and logic. People who came up a revelation like this spent years investigating and researching and then presented it in a ground breaking documentary. You don't just get it by reading a question in a book that contains nothing about the greatest discovery that came when you stopped reading and closed the book!

This was amazing enough but the next thing that flashed through my mind was that Shri Mataji had been that mysterious lady that had appeared on the non-existent television program that I had watched so long ago as a teenager. I felt an incredible joy. Mary had heard my prayers.

It was late at night when I had finished this book and had this major revelation, so I had no one to tell. I thought that this was probably lucky because perhaps I had truly gone stark raving mad and my ability to move around and function was just part of a delusion and not proof that I was OK. I told myself that I probably wouldn't even remember all this in the morning, but I did.

I woke up feeling like I had finally found what I had been unknowingly looking for all my life. I woke up with that feeling I'd known briefly as a child.

It was *that feeling*. The feeling of being one with everything, that ancient feeling – a sense of true belonging, of being a part of everything and everyone, yet owned by no one, and hampered by absolutely nothing. It was as if I had been re united with something that I had lost.

This time *that* feeling stayed. I had finally found it and even more than that, I was united with it. It was a part of my very existence

The biggest smile I'd ever seen spread across Chris's face when I told him what had happened the night that I read that book. At first I thought it was because he thought that I was crazy but it wasn't that at all. It was because I had found the truth.

That night Chris suggested that we went with him to the Friday night program at Burwood which was the main centre for Sahaja. He knew I was planning to visit Lene and Guy, so he thought it would be good for us to go to the program and then meet up with them afterwards. This invitation intrigued me. I couldn't imagine what this place would be like.

Chris told me that it was an ashram. I had no concept of what this would be. I'd only heard stories of abuse and deceit occurring in ashrams through the media as there seemed to be a flood of new age weirdos at this time. I was relieved to know that the ashram was simply a big old house, and that nothing would be any different to what we did each week at Chris's home.

The program was different in one way. Tanaya and I sat at the back of the room. There were about fifty people there of all ages. As soon as we sat down I felt the strongest wave of coolness wash over me. I could say it was unbelievable but that's just it – it was as tangible as a cool breeze swaying a branch. It was very real. This is how the program was different. The cool breeze was so much stronger.

When it finished we looked at the photos of Shri Mataji that were for sale. I let Tanaya choose one for her room as she had become one of Shri Mataji's number one fans. She chose a strange photo of Shri Mataji in a misty atmosphere with what appeared to be two twinkling eyes in the background. I thought that the photo was faulty because of the mist, but Tanaya was determined that this was the one for her. I agreed and went to pay for it. Lene met us there and Tanaya showed her the photo,

"Oh! You recognise it!" exclaimed Lene.

I asked what she meant and she pointed out that the mist and strange twinkling eyes were forming the head of Shri Ganesha, the god that embodies the childhood qualities of innocence and joy. I remembered that a long time ago I had accepted the idea of other gods as my grandmother once told me that she was sure that God must have come to earth many times in all different cultures so that all of humanity could know about unconditional love, but I felt a little uncomfortable with the idea of them actually appearing in a photo. Tanaya just loved it.

We left with Lene and Guy. They lived in a small cottage on the main road of Sydney's North Shore. I had developed a real aversion to such busy places, yet when we entered their home it was as if we were in some idyllic country setting. It wasn't because the décor consisted of open fireplaces, cane baskets and chook motifs but it had everything to do with the atmosphere, or as I was learning to say "It was the vibrations."

I only remember three things that occurred during our stay. The first was looking at photos of Lene and Guy's trip to India while Lene told me of their remarkable journey. Each year in December people who practised this meditation went to India for at least three weeks and travelled all over the country with Shri Mataji and yogis from all over the world. Days were spent travelling to different villages to give self-realisation. The evenings were spent with Shri Mataji listening to her talks, followed by performances from musicians, and performers of all types. It sounded like my idea of a perfect holiday as India was the only country that had ever fascinated me.

The second thing that I remembered was learning a rather odd way to solve problems, called shoe beating. When Lene and Guy explained that we could use the earth to absorb our problems, I thought that this sounded crazy, so you can imagine how I was feeling when I was instructed to use the heel of my left shoe to gently beat the earth. When I look back on all of this, it is truly a miracle in itself that I ever became involved in this Sahaja Yoga because to look at these events without the bigger picture, they all sound totally insane, but I'm telling you, fighting off my nagging criticisms was the best thing I did in my life so if you are thinking of slamming this book shut, don't because this is the truth. It is knowledge of another real dimension. It is like being the first people to hear about people using electricity. Now we all use electricity and eventually we will all use this new dimension.

If you are going to stop reading anyway, then, before you do try re reading the beginning of this chapter with the mind of a scientist but this time actually do the actions as you read. You could get a surprise and find yourself racing to find out more. If you still want to slam this book shut then when you do, turn the book over, flick open the back and google the words listed and read the research articles that have been done that prove the scientifically the benefits of practising Sahaja Yoga.

When Galileo announced that the world was round, everyone thought he was insane yet now it is insane to believe anything else. This is like that.

The third thing that I remember is that Tanaya wouldn't stop crying when it was time to leave and I didn't want to go either. Again Lene gently told us that it was the vibrations that made us not want to leave and not actually their little cottage on the highway.

"Of course," I acknowledged as I consoled Tanaya but I had no idea of how far this new dimension of vibrations would reach into our life.

Tanaya and I kept going to the programs at Chris's place and I kept meditating twice a day for ten minutes and foot soaking at night. To foot soak you just did exactly that. You soaked your feet in a tub of warm salty water whilst sitting on a chair in front of a photo of Shri Mataji with a lit candle in front of it. This was meant to remove all daily stresses and like all things Sahaja I did it with an open mind and it worked.

Chapter 19

Connecting to That Fourth Dimension

By now both Tanaya and I could decipher tingles and heat on our fingers and clear the corresponding chakras or plexuses when we did our morning and evening meditation. When we went home I did include that weird thing called shoe beating. I'd go out at sunset and sit on the hill and write my problems invisibly onto the earth, put an invisible circle around this with my hand and then beat my shoe around it in a clockwise direction one hundred and eight times while I gazed at the sky or the ocean. Every day I would write, "Negativity stopping me from getting a permanent teaching position in the Hunter valley," as this was all I really wanted.

I was sure that if I got a position in the Hunter Valley, I could definitely live with Stephanie and Anne who had bought an old community hall and were slowly transforming it into what they hoped would become an ashram. In Sahaja yoga I had learnt that this simply meant a group of normal people that shared a house, meditated together, went to work and held programs once a week for other people who wanted to learn about Sahaja yoga and all its techniques.

We went to Burwood a few times for programs and we did go to two other ceremonies which were all designed to improve our vibrations and to help to clear negativity of all descriptions, from global warming to war, fanaticism of all kinds, materialism, problems in your job or family life.

The first one was a puja. If you know about Hinduism, you'll know that this is the name of religious Hindu ceremony where they worship one of the gods. This Sahaja one was different to Hinduism. Chris explained that this ceremony was a way of focussing on developing the qualities of one specific chakra and that in order to benefit from it, we should stay in meditation with our eyes open watching what was happening on the stage. After it was over it was important to stay in meditation in order to soak up the vibrations that would flow strongly at the end.

Stephanie had given me a sari and green glass bangles. These were to wear at the puja. I looked down at the sari swooshing around my bare ankles and feet and the glass bangles jingling on my wrists and saw flashes of the feet from my childhood dream-the feet that knew how to run before I could even walk and did so through dirt tracks to half-finished thatched walls to safety. I don't remember much of this puja. I don't even know what chakra we were focussing on.

All I remember was that flash of my dream, the vibrations that were incredibly strong and feeling like I had missed wearing this five and a half metres of fabric that should felt have felt very strange to me. I had also missed the tinkling of glass bangles as they moved around on my wrists. I remember that the three hour ceremony seemed to last no time and it was easy for not just me, but also Tanaya, to sit still cross-legged in meditation for the entire time.

The other ceremony I went to was a havan. Again I don't remember every detail but I'll never forget the moment when I walked out the back door to the gathering for this event. Again you may recognise this as a Hindu practice but to a naïve ex catholic like me it was a mysterious ceremony around a fire where we said ancient mantras and then finished by offering global problems and negativity. It was held in the backyard of the Burwood ashram. When I walked outside I saw the fire and all these angelic faces glowing in its light. All of the women were dressed in colourful saris and some of the men were dressed in traditional Indian men's clothing. I knew in that instant that they were the people that I had seen in my childhood. They were the ones I had caught a glimpse of beyond the horizon that day that I stood with my doll tucked under my arm. They hadn't been at a strange picnic as I thought that day. They were at this havan. This was what I'd seen in that moment.

From that instant on I knew that I had finally come home. I felt that these people were somehow going to help to change the world. I knew that these people and this thing called Sahaja yoga was what I had been trying to find and had nearly missed out on ever discovering.

This was the thread that kept appearing whenever I experienced that elusive feeling. This thread had become a strong visible presence and it had drawn me to make this connection to that other dimension that I had captured glimpses of all my life.

Chapter 20

Shri Mataji's Visit

One day we got the unbelievable news that Shri Mataji would be in Australia to celebrate Easter at a scout camp in Bundilla, Sydney. She was going to arrive in Perth and visit other capital cities before Easter. Tanaya and I couldn't go with the other yogis to meet and travel with her, as she was arriving before the school holidays started. Anyway, we could never afford the air fares to go but we could certainly get to the airport in Sydney to meet her when she arrived there and then go to the Easter celebrations that would definitely include a puja.

Over the following weeks we prepared for her visit by meditating with the yogis from the Newcastle area and working on our own personal imbalances. Only rain would stop me from shoe beating. I was still shoe beating getting a job anywhere in the Hunter Valley and had given until the last day of first term in 1991 before I would improve my employment chances by applying for Sydney as well.

Chris found out that Shri Mataji had one free night whilst in Sydney. At this time Newcastle had the biggest group of Sahaja yogis outside of Sydney. Chris asked Tanaya to write a letter to Shri Mataji inviting her to come to Newcastle. Tanaya was given this job simply because she was the oldest child in our group. She asked Shri Mataji to come to Newcastle because there were "silly people that drank and swore like the ones at the logs" near her house. She said that if Shri Mataji came to Newcastle the vibrations would stop these people from being so silly and she could help everyone by giving them their realisation. We were all happy with this invitation and put it away for safe keeping until Easter when Tanaya would present it to Shri Mataji.

The last week of school arrived. I was so eager to get to the day that Shri Mataji would arrive in Australia that I had forgotten that the end of this week was the deadline I had set for getting a job in the Hunter Valley.

It happened about 9.30am on the last day of school before the Easter holidays. I was called away from my class to take a phone call from the Department of Education. I thought it would just be to check paperwork. I stood in utter disbelief with the phone to my ear as I was offered my first permanent teaching position at Muswellbrook South Public School in the Hunter valley. The person that made the call was just as amazed. He told me that in the fifteen years that he had worked in the department, this was the first time he had offered a job to anyone waiting for their first permanent position in this area. He even told me that the job was definitely meant for me because three other people on the list before me had knocked it back. Apparently this had never happened before either but this time it did and I finally had a permanent job.

This was how I learned the real the power of this shoe beating and also the importance of being very clear on what it is you desired. I did get exactly what I had wanted- a permanent teaching position in the Hunter Valley, but I didn't stop to find out just how big this valley was. As it turned out Muswellbrook was in the Upper Hunter and Stephanie and Anne lived in the Lower Hunter, a good two hours' drive away. It would be impossible to live with these two yogis or to attend their programs. Instead I would be travelling solo as a Sahaja yogi to this country town.

That last day of term was one filled with emotion. We left the school with Tanaya crying along with most of the Year 6 girls who loved both of us. The drama of moving house was put on hold until after Shri Mataji left Newcastle.

We packed our last items ready for the trip to meet Shri Mataji and set off for Sydney to stay at Lene and Guy's place.

We drove to the airport together. We met up with the other yogis who were there. Tanaya and I were each holding a red rose that Ariane, Lene's very sweet Swiss flatmate had given to us to present to Shri Mataji. That airport was stuffy but as soon as Shri Mataji began to approach us, there was an incredible coolness that preceded her. It got stronger the closer she came. The whole atmosphere changed. On our way to the airport I remember feeling as though I was a little girl that was going to meet the real Santa Claus. I was so excited as

I rehearsed what I would say to her if I actually got to give her the rose. Now that she was actually approaching I felt as though I was part of another dimension where emotions and thoughts dissolved.

The moment came when Shri Mataji was really there standing in front of Tanaya and me. She was short and large with a face that beamed. Every word left my mind as I soaked up the coolness of her energy. Shri Mataji looked at me as though she had known me forever. I felt as though I was handing her the flower in slow motion. She smiled and thanked me as she took the rose. She smelt of the perfume that had inexplicably appeared in my bedroom in the weeks of that gnawing feeling that led me to Sahaja. The feeling of being close to her was exactly that feeling that I'd almost forgotten ever knowing. It was that feeling of being a part of everything and everywhere, yet nothing. "I" had ceased to exist.

As we left the airport Ariane asked me how I felt when I gave Shri Mataji the rose. All I could say was that I could not believe that she had thanked me when that was the very thing I needed to say to her but couldn't because somehow I'd become incapable of saying a single word. I was overwhelmed by her simple thanks. I didn't know how Tanaya felt. I didn't even think to ask her.

My next memories are of the camp. Tanaya and I settled in easily. It felt like we were where we truly belonged. Tanaya must have felt like I did when we met Shri Mataji because as soon as we got there she found the little cottage that Shri Mataji was staying in. From then on every spare moment that this little six year old girl had, was spent sitting cross legged in meditation outside that cottage just for the chance to catch a glimpse of this woman that had captured her heart. The image of her sitting there like a little yogi with her back dead straight and her little face glowing is impossible to forget.

That whisper of a feeling was now becoming a constant state of being and getting stronger, ever since we had met Shri Mataji in person. Although, we did not see her until we were all gathered in the huge tent, you could feel her presence. The vibrations were this feeling and now they were so cool- like gentle waves.

The night before the puja I had one of those dreams. I woke up with that feeling except this time it was followed by a feeling of being cocooned in complete love as the memory of this very different kind of dream washed over me.

I had dreamt that Shri Mataji had woken me up and asked me to come to her. I was sitting on my knees a respectable distance away from her but she told me to move closer and indicated to kneel as close to her side as I could. She held my left hand and rubbed my little finger, saying not to be worried or nervous because there would be a havan before the puja to prepare me to come this close to her without the nervous feeling that overwhelmed me in the dream.

Immediately after the final scene of the dream slipped from my mind, one of the organisers was calling out to everyone that Shri Mataji wanted to have a havan before the puja, so we all needed to get ready earlier. There had been no plan to have a havan. It was exactly as she had said.

The havan felt very powerful.

When the puja started, Tanaya went up to wash Shri Mataji's feet with all the other children. The adults participated in the next part. The organiser requested for seven ladies who had never performed puja with Shri Mataji in person, to come to the front. The moment the last syllable was uttered I found myself standing and being ushered forward to the puja area as one that had actually been chosen to do the puja.

I felt as nervous as I had in the dream. I was standing right in front of her and she was looking at me exactly as she had in the dream. She indicated where I was to kneel and it was in the exact position I had taken in the dream. All nerves left me and I just felt thoughtless and empty of all emotion. I offered fruit to her, I painted her feet in the sacred red kum kum powder, I decorated them with toe rings and anklets, I tied on an arm band and I put delicate glass bangles around her wrists. During the whole ceremony I was in another dimension. I had that wonderful sensation that I had yearned for as a child and it was changing my life. I also felt I was with Mary.

Later, I learnt that it is most unusual to omit the word "married" from the request for ladies to do the puja. It was just as

Chris had told me that wherever you sit or whatever part you play in this ceremony, it was meant to happen. Had they made the usual request I would not have been able to take part. It was as if that dream was literally Shri Mataji preparing me to do that puja.

I knew I had found my true family and I felt that somehow this woman was truly saving the world. After all, everything that I had experienced through her yoga had transformed me, and it is said that if one person is changed then the world is changed. She was changing thousands all over the world.

Shri Mataji accepted Tanaya's invitation and came to Newcastle to the Town Hall to give a public program. My mother and a few friends came to the program with me. Once more, I related to every word that she uttered. It was as if she was speaking only to me, answering even more of the questions that I had ever asked about life and where we were all heading. I soaked up every word.

At the end of the program she asked for anyone who had never met her in person to come up and see her. Mum wouldn't go unless I came with her. The long line seemed to quickly shorten and mum and I were kneeling in front of her.

Again Shri Mataji took my left hand and stroked it but this time she also stroked my little finger with a little more pressure. She did this the whole time we were with her. At the time I had no idea of the significance of this action.

She looked at my mother saying, "So this is your mother? Look. She feels it. Look into her eyes. See the light that shines in her eyes? She feels it."

When I looked at my mother's eyes I saw them sparkling with the clearest blue and two deep shining pupils. She was glowing. She looked like a sweet, innocent little girl. I nodded my head in response.

From that day on the relationship with my mother completely changed. It had been very difficult. Now it was a perfect one. How did this happen? The left hand represented my past and my little finger on the left hand was connected to the relationship that I had with my mother. Shri Mataji had felt the pain of our relationship without even knowing us. She had felt our vibrations. By that simple gesture of just stroking my hand, Shri Mataji removed the past hurt and so, changed our relationship.

I thought about this experience and realised that my childhood revelation was true. Thoughts were completely different to experience and this is exactly what had happened. We had both been a part of a very pure experience. It had been a crystal clear reality. This simple experience had transformed how we saw each other.

Shri Mataji's energy felt so powerful. With one look she was able to see your inner being and completely erase any thought that you were trying to put together.

When the weekend finished Lene and Guy took us back to their house for a few days. A strange sensation came over me as we drove down the Pacific Highway back to Chatswood. I felt as though I had been away for years but we had only been at the camp for three days. Everything felt so different. This was another interesting quality of the time spent in this woman's presence. Hours seemed like days and a minute could be an eternity. It was definitely another dimension. Once again no one told me that this would happen. I hadn't read it anywhere it just simply happened. I had *experienced* it.

When I mentioned it to Lene and Guy they knew exactly what I was talking about.

Chapter 21

Muswellbrook and Miracles

Tanaya and I moved to Muswellbrook a week after that heavenly weekend. Our new home was a three bedroom cottage complete with air conditioning. It had a beautiful garden and was a vast improvement on the small one bedroom flat that was our home in Redhead. Our neighbour had six children so Tanaya's wish to have friends next door to play with definitely came true.

My new job was everything I had wished for. I got on well with our principal, and more importantly with my new class. Tanaya loved her new school. She improved in all her subjects and even proved to be a talented athlete. Thankfully she was not at all like me in the arena of athleticism.

Before getting my self-realisation I couldn't even think about moving to a new area or starting a new job without feeling as though my heart would jump out of my chest with intense anxiety. It was incredible to be in a remote country town knowing no body and feeling so relaxed about it.

At the end of our first school day, Tanaya and I went shopping. I wished that I could have a cup of tea and a chat with some of our new Sahaja friends. It would have been the perfect ending to that day. We were walking up the main street when I saw the sign indicating the number of miles to Tamworth. It seemed to gently remind me that seeing any yogi would be impossible as they were all so far away.

We stood at the only set of traffic lights in town, and waited to cross the highway as trucks carrying pigs and a stream of utes drove by. I was staring at the ground, when something that wasn't a green light made me look up slightly. Glass bangles around both wrists of the person in front of me made my heart sing. I looked up and poked my head around to see the person's face.

She was wearing a Sahaja yoga badge.

"Excuse me but are you Sahaja yogis," I asked.

"Yes," answered a surprised voice. I blurted out who I was and how I had been wishing for yogis' company. I could have saved my breath because they recognised me from Burwood and one of them was even Lene's friend. We walked together to the nearest café.

"Now I know why Joseph wouldn't stop at the last place. What was it called?" Lindsay asked her husband, Joseph.

"Scone" answered Emma, as Joseph was talking with Tanaya.

"We were dying to stop but he just kept driving and said that we would stop at the next town. We couldn't believe it! Joseph just kept driving and said he didn't know why we were going to the next town. It just didn't feel right to stop. We didn't even know what the next town was!"

"The poor things" I thought, "It's a forty minute drive from here."

"See we had to come and meet Lisa", Joseph joined in with a broad grin.

We enjoyed a coffee together, and the chat I had wanted whilst Tanaya slurped on a milkshake. What they had told me stunned me and showed me once more how vibrations worked. These vibrations were definitely a mothering energy because they knew your heart felt desire and fulfilled it as long it was good for you. This is just what a mother does. This energy was a reality and not something concocted by the desire for something more than what we know. Once again I was shown that Sahaja yoga was experiences and not a lot of new age visualising.

Tanaya and I lived the life of locals with the exception of our ten minute meditation morning and night, a bit of private shoe beating and a few trips away to join in with other yogis for pujas or just a get together. I was amazed at how many coincidences filled our life and then I reminded myself that these were not coincidences but rather these gentle but powerful vibrations "working it out" and trying to fulfil our desires , just to remind us that they were there waiting to help us if we could only remember this. It's a hard thing to turn off a mind used to worrying and trying to find answers.

Funny isn't it? It is hard to stop worrying and accept a very simple solution that involves doing very little at all. You'd think that the human mind would jump at a chance to have a rest!

My first year at Muswellbrook South public school ended with both Tanaya and I feeling very satisfied. This was something I had never experienced.

Early in January, Tanaya and I returned to Burwood. The lucky group that had gone on India Tour had returned with wonderful stories of travelling with Shri Mataji, and all the sights and sounds of India. I literally began to crave to be there. My good old brain kept telling me that it was crazy to take leave without pay when I had only just started fulltime employment. My vibrations were telling me something quite different. I put all this out of my mind as it was so far into the future. The school holidays ended and Tanaya and I returned to Muswellbrook to get on with our school lives. I found myself wishing for another experience like Easter puja.

My wish was granted with a letter from Chris. It was an invitation to come to another puja with Shri Mataji at Glenrock Lagoon. She was coming to my home territory as this was just a five minute drive from where I had grown up. I couldn't believe it and I rushed to accept the invitation. The puja was in the holidays so it was perfect in every way. When we arrived, a lady that we had met once before greeted us and immediately took me into the little cottage that Shri Mataji was to stay in. She asked me to help arrange flowers for Shri Mataji's room while Tanaya played with the other children.

The next day yogis went to the beach to foot soak. I walked down to where they were.

I stood in the ocean thoughtless and just drank in this incredible scene that was taking place right near where I had lived. It was like that scene from one of my teenage dreams. I was beginning to understand that those dreams had also taken me into another dimension that was the future.

This puja was even more powerful than the first one. Some yogis even had to leave Shri Mataji's presence as the vibrations had become so strong. Once more Shri Mataji seemed to just talk to me. She even spoke about ecological problems. After Shri Mataji had spoken to us Tanaya washed Shri Mataji's feet along with all the other children and I just sat in blissful meditation, relieved from all thoughts. The vibrations were strong and cool.

The biblical quote, "The cool breeze of the Holy Spirit" came to mind.

Tanaya and I returned to Muswellbrook completely rejuvenated. Once again it felt as though we had been away for years.

Sometimes I would find myself incredibly short of money, as we all do. On one of those occasions Tanaya and I wanted to travel from Muswellbrook to Newcastle, then on to Redhead; back to Newcastle and then on to Sydney for our program at Burwood. This was roughly a three hundred and fifteen kilometre trip, but I only had ten dollars' worth of petrol. I just had to go and I would not ask for money from anyone. I remembered another strange Sahaja technique that I had been told about and decided to give it a go.

Before we left, I meditated and when my thoughts stopped, I gave the problem a bandhan. This was a very simple technique of writing a problem on your left hand invisibly with your finger and then circling around it with your right hand until it felt cool. I can tell exactly what you are thinking. It's exactly the same as I thought when I was told about it. It's crazy! It sounded so bizarre that I didn't even bother to try it until this occasion, almost two years after I had gotten my realization. I tried it because every other unbelievable thing I had been told to do in Sahaja had worked and I was desperate and determined.

We stayed with yogis when we reached Newcastle. The petrol tank was almost on empty. In the morning, after meditation, I went out to the car to get something. I quickly forgot what it was, when I saw a puddle of petrol in the gutter beside my car.

On closer inspection, it seemed that petrol was leaking out of my tank. Devastated at the possibility of losing the precious little petrol I had left, I rang roadside service while my bewildered friend guarded the car. I was a bit worried that a smoker might walk past and flick a lit butt towards the petrol puddle.

When I came back, I moved the car away from the puddle for safety's sake and then took off the petrol cap. What I saw should have been absolutely impossible. As soon as I took the cap off, a little fountain of petrol spurted up about ten centimetres above the opening of the petrol tank. I quickly put the cap back on, in shock.

The roadside attendant came quickly. When he removed the petrol cap, the petrol began to spurt up like a fountain again. It honestly was a petrol fountain! The attendant asked me to move the car to the flat where he could accurately measure the pressure in the tank because he thought that this phenomenon was caused by an air lock in the tank. He tested his theories using every tool possible. Finally he just stood up, looked at me and told me that I simply had far too much petrol in my tank. I explained that this was not possible because I had only been able to put ten dollars' worth of petrol in my tank when I left Muswellbrook. I told him that was with my last ten dollars so I was more than sure of how much I had bought and then I'd come here, gone to Redhead and returned. This was a journey of around one hundred and fifty-four kilometres.

He looked at me with frustration and a little irritation saying, "You mean that you filled up down the road here when you returned because the tank is simply way overfilled."

As the miraculous fountain of petrol continued to gently bubble, I repeated what I had said I'd done.

Finally, he looked at me in utter disbelief and frustration and said, "Well love, I don't know what you used to get here or what you are playing at. It must have been thin air; because I'm telling you, the only thing wrong with your car is that it has too much petrol."

He had to siphon off some of it to stop the fountain. All of our needs were met those holidays and I never doubted the power of a bandhan again!

The time came for those making the trip to India to start making arrangements. This was going to be a six week trip because fares were cheaper if they left earlier and the Indian yogis in Delhi had arranged accommodation there until the tour officially began. This made my desire to join this tour even stronger. I had the airfare so no matter how hard my brain was trying to tell me that to go to India was nonsense, I was going to go. I just had to let these vibrations work out anything stopping this from happening.

The first obstacle to reaching India was to get leave without pay which was not, at that stage easily granted. I was going to apply for it when the time to go came closer. One lunchtime, we had a staff meeting with the region's staff welfare officer. When I asked him about the possibility of this leave, he told me that he would support it, but I was nearly out of time to apply. It was no coincidence that he had come at that particular time to talk to us! I filled out the paperwork and the leave was granted.

The only other obstacle was to ask my parents to mind Tanya over Christmas. This bothered me more than getting leave from school, as Christmas was still a very special time to our family and it meant just that- family. Again, it worked out very easily. My parents had seen what a difference Sahaja yoga had made to me and mum had felt the power of being in Shri Mataji's presence. They agreed.

The path was cleared for the trip of a lifetime. Sahaja yogi's called Shri Mataji, Mother. They had always told me that the mothering energy that she had enabled us to connect to would take care of everything. I was learning just how true this was.

There was one huge obstacle that I never saw coming. A few weeks before I was due to leave, I was walking back to class after lunch when I stepped into a hole covered with grass. I fell and felt agonizing pain shoot into my left ankle. It swelled up immediately, and the pain along with the swelling stayed. I went to the local doctor who thankfully knew nothing about my leg history. With the use of inner soles discreetly worn in flat shoes, I was able to walk around as a normal person.

Now I had to let him know and at the worst possible time. I told him the story and about my plans to go to India. He gave me a referral for an x ray and told me that I would have to cancel my plans. My heart sank, but I refused to even consider the possibility of cancelling my trip as I hobbled out of his office on crutches. Thoughtless awareness was a must then or I would have crumbled into a crying mess.

I was still in pain when I headed back to the doctor to get results of the x-rays. I was about to find out that nothing gets in the way of a pure desire once that connection to this mothering energy is made.

When I got to the surgery, I was told that my usual doctor had taken unexpected leave. He was replaced by an Indian Doctor. In the entire seven years that I lived in Muswellbrook I never again saw an Indian doctor at that surgery, as a matter of fact I don't think there was even an Indian person in the whole town. This doctor broke the news to me about the small fracture that I had in my left ankle. He suggested that it should be plastered but he was not at all like the previous doctor.

I took a deep breath and explained to him that this couldn't happen as I was going to India no matter what. He quizzed me as to why I wanted to go. I told him the whole story. He understood my determination to go to his home country no matter what. Amazingly, he even agreed not to plaster my ankle but to strap it, if I agreed to use crutches up until I left for India, in about three weeks.

He smiled and told me to enjoy his country.

As much as I couldn't believe my luck in not having it plastered, I also couldn't believe how unlucky I had been. It was difficult enough to teach with crutches, let alone prepare for India tour.

One weekend I was staying at my parents' house so that we could spend some together before I left for India. I had to finish shopping for the trip while I was there because I couldn't get everything I needed in Muswellbrook. One night I meditated and gave the whole thing a bandhan as I was totally fed up with pain and trying to hobble around.

That night I had a dream that was at the same time a reality. I dreamt that I was in India with my mother. I could see everything so clearly. Mum and I were with all the yogis somewhere in the mountains. Below us flowed a beautiful jade river, edged with spectacular white quartz boulders.

We were all looking down at this breathtaking scene, when Shri Mataji appeared beside me and said, "Come with me and I will show you how to fix this ankle."

We walked away from everyone and sat down together under a tree. She told me to look into my ankle. I could see a black mark on the fractured bone. It was not like looking at flesh and it was not like looking at an x-ray. It was a different vision to what we normally have. Shri Mataji began to massage my ankle by pushing down on it, using the upper part of her palm and ending with the heel of her hand. It was a rolling motion. She asked me to follow her with my palm. We did this until the black spot disappeared. Then she told me to go back to the others. I did and that was the end of the dream. I slept through that entire night without even waking. Usually my painful ankle would wake me up demanding a new position in the bed but it didn't that night.

I had none of the usual morning pain in my ankle. I tested it out, daring to put all my weight on it to walk without the crutches. All the pain and swelling had gone. I walked into the lounge room where my mother was. She just looked at me with a stunned look on her face. I thought that this was because I could walk on my ankle, so I began to explain how I had the most amazing dream about Shri Mataji and India.

I didn't get a chance to go any further, as mum's stunned silence ended.

"Tell me about it! I must have been with you. I'm worn out. I've been a nervous wreck! I dreamt that I was in India with all these people and Shri…Shri…Whatever her name is…Oh I know, Shri Mataji was supposed to be there but she went off somewhere with you and as usual I couldn't find you anywhere. I was a nervous wreck trying to stop all these people from going too close to the edge of this mountain to see a river. I thought that they would fall off! I told them that this was not Australia and that there were no safety rails that would save them if the edge gave way. I had a terrible time!" poor mum babbled.

I could hardly take in what I was hearing. Somehow, my mother had come with me on this miraculous dream. My mother could hardly believe her eyes when she had calmed down enough to realize I was standing there without crutches.

"What are you doing? Where are your crutches!" were mum's next incredulous words.

I gently explained that we had been in the same dream together. I explained that when I left her with all those people too close to the edge of the ridge, I had gone with Shri Mataji so that she could show me how to heal my ankle. I was so lucky that mum believed in miracles. She simply accepted this as fact and we marveled over it at the breakfast table with tea and toast.

That day I shopped until the shops were all closed, and not one twinge of pain came to my ankle. It *was* a miracle.

When I went back to work, the librarian spotted me walking to the office. When I began working in Muswellbrook, she had asked me about Sahaja yoga as soon as she tracked me down as the owner of the car with the Sahaja sticker. This sophisticated librarian, who had even supped tea with the queen, came to my house to get her self- realisation and to learn how to meditate. She felt the vibrations of this other dimension and loved it

When she saw me she called out excitedly, "What has happened?"

I didn't know how to answer. I knew I had to tell her the amazing truth but not by calling out across the playground so I went up to her and explained the whole story.

She beamed at me when I asked her if she thought I was crazy and just said, "I know it's true. I can see for myself. It's a real living miracle!"

It was reassuring to be able to share what had happened with someone as levelheaded as this woman because it gave me more proof that it was a reality. I wasn't crazy.

I still kept waiting for my ankle to give out or for me to wake up, but neither happened.

I was going to India.

Chapter 22

Finding the Reality of Dreams

I was still afraid of flying as well as road trips, crossing busy roads without a crossing or lights, the thought of war, having an accident of any kind and sport or any other kind of game. It was amazing that I ever managed to leave the house never mind have fun. Sahaja had enabled me to overcome many of my fears but those ones had refused to budge. Thankfully I didn't feel the paralyzing fear I had felt when I flew to New Zealand as we boarded the plane to fly to India. I felt calm and protected. I amazed myself.

When the flight began, I had managed to stay relaxed and enjoyed watching the people I was to spend the next six weeks with. I listened to the voices around me until sleep took over. I remember waking up to what felt like a bumpy ride in a car. For a moment, all my childhood fear of crashing in a plane tried to come back, until I shook off sleep and reminded myself that we were all protected on our way to India and that this sensation was called turbulence. After a few shaky moments that felt like hours, I managed to become centered once more. I also knew that I could use the power of that strange simple thing called a bandhan for even more protection.

Our stopover was in Singapore.

Singapore airport seemed unreal to me as we walked through its vastness that was beautifully decorated with orchids. Queensland yogis greeted us and gave each of us one of those exquisite flowers. They had all arrived on an earlier flight.

We arrived at the motel that night exhausted. After a meal and exchanging our money, we meditated in our rooms and went to sleep, or tried to. A constant banging and whirring of the air conditioner and incredible heart palpitations made it impossible for me. These palpitations stayed with me for the entire time that we were in Singapore but they didn't really bother me. The old me would have been sure I was facing an impending sudden death by heart failure. The only time I was concerned was when my heart reached an almost painful crescendo in response to an unwelcome phone call in the early hours of the morning that jolted us all from whatever rest we were managing. It was a creepy call with a man wanting to know our ages and asking if we would like to go to a party. Another of my childhood fears was that I would be murdered in my sleep, or at a party. This fear came from being far too young to read a newspaper's vivid description of a brutal murder in a home close to where we were staying in Sydney. The images I created whilst reading that brutal article stayed locked away in my memories and now they had tried to face me. Incredibly I just saw it as a rude interruption. That was all it was really. Although it could have been more if we had accepted this eerie invitation. In the morning we read the motel information that warned guests of these calls that targeted party going westerners to drug them and rob them of passports and money. The old me would have been petrified even though the experience had long gone. Instead I just listened to the information as it was read out and continued to prepare for our day in Singapore, my first experience of Asia.

Mamta, one of my room mates came from Singapore and had grown up in the area that we were staying in, so she took us on a guided tour to the local market where we feasted on foods that looked and smelt like nothing I'd ever seen before. We feasted on pawpaw, sour sop juice, chestnut juice, pork and chicken dumplings and some kind of cake which was supposed to be carrot cake but when our faces reacted to its hot flavour our chuckling hosts told us via Mamta that it was radish!

One of the stall holders asked Mamta had she shipped us all from Australia because it was unusual for any tourists to go there let alone a group as big as ours. Everyone that we met found us Aussies quaint. Smiles and laughter were everywhere. After breakfast we visited another small market filled with intriguing produce as we made our way to meet the other yogis who had been on a shopping spree of a more expensive nature. At one intersection along the way something made me look up.

There on top of the building across the road was a magnificent scene of larger than life fairies and pure white horses. As soon as I looked at them they came to life, moving to beautiful music. I felt like a small child taken away on a magic carpet as I gazed upwards at this scene which wished us all a "Christmas of Inspiration." I felt like a small child but I thought nothing. I was just in the bliss that is Sahaja.

We met the others in a very western shopping centre. After our lunch, a few of us went shopping. I just enjoyed eating cakes that I had never seen and the tastes were certainly like nothing I had ever tried. It was all fantastic. The greatest treasures that I brought away with me were the memories of the Christmas decorations, none of which included Santa, elves or reindeer. Instead there were swans, candles, horses, fairies and messages of peace and joy. All of these reminded passersby of the true message of Christmas unlike most of our decorations at home which all seemed designed to make us all want more and so take us further away from the original message of love and peace.

We arrived back at the motel hot and exhausted. Mamta excitedly chatted to her old friends in the foyer. I marvelled at how in all of Singapore we had picked a motel in Mamta's hometown. You could call it coincidence but I was learning there is no such thing in life and that there would always be plenty of them. As we left for the final leg of our journey, I felt as though I had become a part of a movie, and it was going to the best one ever. When we waited to board the plane, the reality of going to India sank in as I looked around at turban headed men smoking cigars, salwar kameez or sari clad women and laughing children dressed in the sweetest dresses.

When the plane took off, those palpitations stopped. I mentioned this to Prue who was sitting next to me and she explained that each country has its own vibrations and sometimes we could actually feel them.

Delhi airport was a stark contrast to Singapore's. My first impression was the smell. It wasn't unpleasant it was just different. Unlike the palpitations that I had in Singapore, I felt a great relief. It felt like it was the place I had been so desperate to find.

After a long wait for luggage, we left the security of the airport and entered the swarming mass of humanity that is India.

People held boards with the names of the people that they were to meet and pushed to get a view of the new arrivals. One person held a sign that read 'Society of Lepers". When I saw him, I also saw how different this society was going to be to ours. The next example of this difference was waiting near our bus. A beggar or maybe a pick pocket came close to our group. A police man blasting on a whistle, approached him, and began to beat him with his long cane as he dragged him away from us. By then the poor man was like a cowering dog. The old me, before the discovery of this thing called thoughtless awareness, would have been sobbing at the sight of this utter cruelty to another person. Instead I watched it without thinking. It didn't mean I felt it was a good thing that I had witnessed. I just didn't react with tears. An older more experienced yogi explained that the policeman had done this to protect us from being robbed. When I remembered how naïve I was about human nature, it was just as well as I encountered this first or I would have been robbed hand over fist during the tour.

I have no idea how long the bus trip was to Hazrat Nizamuddin Scout Camp which was to be our new home for the next few weeks. I remember smiling to myself as the reality of it all sank in deeper, with each jolt of the bus and the weaving of cars and rickshaws. I began to overcome my fear of car accidents when I realized that a horn certainly didn't mean impending death but rather just a way of saying, "I am coming through". It was like a strange dance with every car moving in response to the music of horns rather than to any code of road rules or so it seemed.

We drove past humpies, cows and amazing sights too countless to recall. When the bus turned down a quiet smaller road a wave of vibrations swept over me and my travelling companion Helja asked if I could feel them. I was speechless because I wasn't *feeling* the vibrations. They had become me and I was experiencing that wonderful childhood experience of being a part of everything, everywhere and even everyone yet owned by no one, not anyone, and hampered by absolutely nothing. That this happened then, was incredible, as I had always been petrified of travelling and I was also a complete outsider by normal measures to the environment that I had become one with. This sought after childhood experience was definitely a part of my pure existence because it had even made its presence felt here so far from home

We stopped out the front of igloo shaped buildings. The more experienced travellers exclaimed that we had luxury accommodation when they saw metal double bunks with very old worn mattresses on some. They were the only furnishings in our little cement floored huts. Unlike Singapore I fell asleep very quickly that night, still wrapped in that wonderful experience of oneness and *that feeling*.

The sound of distant horns woke me during the night and it hit me how far I was from Tanaya. I realised how attached I was to her and how much I already missed her. Thoughts tried to turn this into emotional drama but I turned my attention to the top of my head and once again experienced sleep. The next time I opened my eyes it was to the sound of a distant voice singing songs of worship to Allah and dawn.

At this time in my journey I did not even know that this was a Muslim singing the call to prayer nor was I aware of the conflict between Hindus and Muslims in some areas of India. In fact I was incredibly oblivious to any facts of India. I was just completely absorbed with experiencing India and knowing only about this ancient feeling of another dimension that had stayed with me.

We all seemed to wake up together to prepare for meditation. We all left our little hut together. The air was thick with smog and it was chilly. I had never seen smog and it reminded me of the thick mists that our family loved in the Blue Mountains. I am not going to describe every meditation that we had on this tour because it would be boring and it is impossible to describe these meditations as there were no words that came in thoughts during that entire time so there is nothing to recall, except to say that it was an experience of being one with everything; being nothing yet everywhere. This experience gave a feeling of lightness and joy that we all must lose somewhere on the path that takes us out of childhood. This experience and feeling stayed with me long after meditations finished. It had become a part of me.

Our Indian hosts prepared us a western breakfast of simple omelettes, bread, jam and banana washed down with hot chocolate. This was followed by a meeting to discuss essential information about our camp, such as the need for security. A group of Aussies staying in a scout camp somewhere in Delhi for weeks alone could find themselves vulnerable to theft. Armed security guards at our door assured absolute security.

The good news was that the Sahaja yogis in Delhi were going to look after us completely until the international tour began. They were going to take care of everything including providing enough bottled water on site for us to buy, taking care of our laundry, providing information about anything we wished to know about, hiring buses to take us out for shopping for bargains at quality markets, not to mention feeding us with beautiful meals and spoiling us with that unexpected hot chocolate.

There were certain facts we were told that no one could afford to be oblivious to such as carrying passport and valuables with you under your clothing at all times. Actually, carrying is the wrong word, it was actually wearing it and at all times meant just that. The only time I dared to take off my leather pouch of valuables was when I had a bath, and sometimes I dared to leave it off when I was sleeping and put it inside and at the bottom of my sleeping bag. This was the first of those vital facts that I learnt quickly and never forgot. After our meeting which felt to me more like a family gathering, a group of us set off to exchange money at a motel within walking distance.

There was only one road to cross and my state of thoughtless awareness was blown away with the first horn blast. The one road we had to cross looked like a raging torrent of people, animals and machinery. Grace who I hardly knew until this moment, suddenly become my protector as she saw my fear and just grabbed me by the arm like a mother does a child to make a quick safe dash across the road. I was shaking when we got to the other side but Grace just smiled and told me how she had been the same in her first trip to this land of the spirit. It seemed that the most spiritual place on earth was filled with so much to learn in order to take care of the physical before I could focus on the spiritual.

The day took on the mundane when we reached the motel and everyone that wanted money exchanged learnt quickly that it wasn't possible. An Indian yogi who was married to an Australian, was sweetly trying to stay in the centre and help his western brothers and sisters whose spirituality had been smothered as they all tried to point out that their credit card was accepted everywhere or that they only needed a small amount of cash. I felt a bit embarrassed as I watched how quickly things had unravelled over money. If we all needed money for food or to put a roof over our heads, then this situation would be serious, but we didn't because as I said earlier we were being taken care of completely. The concept of no money seemed impossible for some to understand. The entire drama lasted half an hour. I wouldn't have remembered it but I was so stunned by the transformation that had occurred over money I wrote it in my diary.

Grace mothered me across the road again and back to our camp. We ate lunch watching little chipmunk creatures playing while eagles soared in the sky. Rest followed but I used the time to write in my diary. I had never kept one, or at least not since my mother found my teenage one and grounded me forever. Stephanie and Anne had ensured that I was thoroughly prepared for my trip and that included packing a diary. Stephanie had told me that Shri Mataji had suggested that we keep one. I couldn't really see the importance of this until now. When you are completely steeped in nothing but vibrations, it isn't that you can't remember things so much, but that there are so many unforgettable experiences that they all become a blur.

I didn't manage to write each week never mind daily. I just managed to write enough to capture these times and to form the skeleton of this book.

"It's another world" is a worn out phrase but this time it is being used to state a fact because this India tour was truly another world. I still honestly recorded the fact that at times I was frightened but it lasted only momentarily until the state of that special feeling took me back into that other dimension and the next time I wrote in the diary was one week later. I wrote the same as I write here. You cannot begin to explain what life was like.

Everyday things changed such as "the porcelain throne" was demoted to a hole in the ground over which you squatted; city roads never looked safe; and beggars and hawkers were everywhere. New facts had to be learned to deal with these new versions of everyday things. Some of these were: toilet paper does not exist but water for washing does; never give money to a beggar as you will be swamped by many more; don't look at persistent beggars or hawkers but instead put your hand up in a stop sign and unlike the traffic they will stop: walk boldly to cross the road or you could miss your entire days outing if you stood and waited for a break in the traffic.

The next day Helja, a Finnish yogi who I had met in Sydney, took me to do some shopping. First we had to get some travellers cheques cashed. I knew this would be a long process because there were no dole payments in India and employment had remained a priority here. This meant a simple bank transaction involved the employment of three workers; one to site the cheque and give you a form to complete; one to check the form with the cheques signature and a final one to do a last signature check and to give the money. Incredibly long queues also meant a long wait.

I was prepared to wait the two hours it had taken to get to the final checking stage, but I wasn't prepared to be told that my signature was, "Far too small, madam and could not possibly be your true signature."

We were in the Bank of India; a rundown monsoon marked wooden building with armed army type security guards that seemed to stand on full alert. It was hot and hence my tiny signature had become a little smudged as we stood in that sweaty queue. I was resigned to the fact I would have to wait another day when Helja spotted the familiar letters ANZ on a bank standing proudly amongst India's cityscape.

We went inside to an air conditioned marble bank complete with lush indoor gardens. In no time I was sitting in a luxurious velvet armchair until I was pointed in the direction of the smiling teller waiting to hand me over the desired cash. I walked out as if I'd dreamt the entire experience.

Helja smiled at me and asked as we darted between the traffic, "Now Lisa, describe for me an Indian bank."

I certainly understood the enormity of her question because the answer summed up India. Banks could be extreme contrasts of exactly the same thing standing side by side, or around the corner and giving exactly the same service. After this banking adventure, Helja and I snuck into a resort called the Imperial Hotel and drank coffee. Helja even ate fish and chips much to the amusement of some European women. This was yet another stark contrast. The hotel was built like an English mansion. The menus on the table had "Life is a garden party" written as the slogan. The view from our table looked as if it was the perfect setting for such a party, with lush green lawns on which white lacy rort iron tables and chairs and small gazebos were laid out in perfect English style.

That night, back at our camp we enjoyed a musical night by the blazing fire. There were around four hundred of us by then from Finland, Romania, Canada, USA, Japan, Iran, France and South Africa and many other places. The accents of such a variety of languages reminded me of the music of language that I'd imagined as a child except now that moment was transferred into reality as I bathed in language's melody without understanding a word.

During the first week of our tour, we attended two Sahaja yoga public programmes. These were the Indian version of the programs that were held at Charlestown library except that in this spiritual country thousands turned out to get their realisation because in India self-realisation is common knowledge and to achieve this was nearly every Indian's dream. Some wouldn't even dare dream of it as it was historically reserved for only the greatest souls identified by a guru. The opportunity for them to receive it easily and on mass meant no one stayed at home. The greatest difference to our little programs was that Shri Mataji was there in person. Both these programs were very long and spoken in Hindi. Although I have no knowledge of Hindi, the lecture sounded like music and somehow my spirit seemed to understand as I could feel my kundalini moving in response to each word.

Both trips to the programs were by bus and through more contrasting scenes. I saw the worst squalor and poverty beside the most beautiful monument or motel that I could ever imagine. The smell of India was unique. It was the smell of humanity in all its realms. When we reached both venues for the programs, a fairy tale scene awaited us. A huge pendal was filled with tiny lights absolutely everywhere. The pendal for the second program took a couple of minutes to walk from one end to the next.

This was the first time I saw Sahaja yoga in an international context. Here Shri Mataji was known by everyone -Sahaja or not it didn't matter. Bookstores would try to entice you to buy their wares by producing notes that were meant to be written by the woman herself, as soon as they saw our Sahaja badge. We all wore these badges just as conference participants wear theirs- a simple way to see who's who.

I was continually impressed at how our Indian hosts ensured that every little detail was taken care of for us. We were treated like royalty. We ate magnificent food that people stayed up all night to prepare. The food was not at all hot or too spicy because our hosts, under Shri Mataji's guidance, had even taken into consideration our western taste buds. As soon as the buses returned from any outing a cup of hot chai, or soup, would magically appear for everyone, even when our numbers had swelled to over four hundred.

Before the tour officially began, they organised tours for us to visit Mahatma Ghandi's ashram where he took his last breath and the amazing Qutab Minar, the tallest tower in India including the tomb and college with inscriptions that dated back to 4 BC. As soon as we reached this tower and alighted from the bus, I had a rush of memories too fast to recall with the exception of the feeling of that childhood nightmare of running from rocks. This was accompanied by a rush of vibrations forcing their way up the left side of my body and just leaving. Helja was standing beside me. She asked intuitively if I had somehow recognised this place. I whispered that I felt as though I had been here, knowing this was impossible. I recognised it but in reality I knew nothing of this place. Helja and I then stood silently listening to the guide telling us of its history. He told us that in 1369, a lightning strike destroyed the top storey of this tower. I wondered if maybe I had been there and fled. Perhaps this was that crushing nightmare. Perhaps it was the remnants of the last few moments of a past life. There were more deja vue experiences to come.

Later we drove through those villages where the huts had walls made from woven plants that didn't meet the ceilings. I gasped when I recognised that this again was somewhere I had visited in my childhood dreams. This is where I had run to. As I watched this village flash by through the bus window, vibrations rushed up my left side and left me again. Once again Helja noticed this and asked if I knew this place as well. This time I could tell her what I was experiencing. She asked if there was anywhere else that I had dreamed of. When I described the larger than life statues that I enjoyed walking around, she said that this was a place that they often visited on India tour but we weren't going there this time. I smiled and thought how I had been there many times. Helja also explained that the vibrations I had described were clearing out the emotions of my past through the left channel or left side. It made sense.

We visited magnificent parliament house with its sixteen miles of corridors, and the breathtaking Baha'i temple that was built to resemble a closed lotus. We didn't enter the temple but just looked in awe from a distance. I vividly remember the Indian heat as I stood there and I can still feel Helja pulling up my long scarf as she told me to use it cover my head. As I did it she told me I looked like a Muslim woman. I asked Helja what that meant. How naïve I was. I knew nothing of different religions except for my Nar mentioning them as all being from the same God. I remember Helja telling me that in some areas it wasn't good to wear a scarf like that and in others it wasn't good to wear a bindi which I had learnt was the name of the red dot that Hindus wear on their foreheads. I understood this even less and for once didn't even want to ask a million questions to find out. Had I asked the question I may not have liked the answer.

We visited a children's museum. I did not even know they existed. We took a ride in a miniature steam train and played on playground equipment that were based on laws of physics. That was a breathtaking day filled with surprises.

On one of these magical days in Delhi a group of us went shopping with the Indian women to the emporiums. The bus was filled with characters and I'm sure some of our Indian sisters would have loved to have run away from trying to keep us all together and running on time. I had bonded with an Indian yogi from Delhi called Nupur. She was one of our shopping guides. She was more like my personal assistant. She helped me to choose bangles, a silvar kameez or Punjabi as we call had called them and a shawl for Tanaya.

When we got back to our little home, I decided to stay there as my ankle was very sore. The guilt from shopping must have caused this because once again it was my left ankle. I now knew that different chakras were also represented in different parts of our body and not just our hands. The left ankle meant the left Vishuddhi and one thing that would cause it to go out of balance or in this case ache, was that destructive feeling of guilt. Stress from a guilt ridden left Vishuddhi had settled there. I was beginning to realise this guilt had affected my whole life.

Sophie had also stayed behind to collect some clothes from a tailor in the local Muslim market. I went with her as she had assured me there would be no walking. I could just sit in the trishaw, enjoy the ride and wait for her to collect her clothes.

It was a mad ride to get there as we sped along in that trishaw bumping into a black sheep along the way and brushing past all kinds of goodies packed on the stalls we wove through. Sights sped past like a dreamy kaleidoscope made up of hundreds of Muslim men kneeling and bowing in prayer; Berkar clad women whisking through the streets on their way to prayer; staring children; dogs, goats, sheep and more amazing goods for sale. Later when we had returned to the serenity of our little dome, our Indian brothers and sisters came with that wonderful hot chocolate and supper cooked just for us.

Chapter 23

It Came Without Wrapping

It was my birthday. At 4.00 am we were all awakened by a little bugle calling us to meditate. The very moment I sat up in bed, all of my new Sahaja sisters, sang "Happy birthday."

Prue gave me a small stainless steel cup filled with jelly beans, Helja gave me an Indian "survival" kit consisting of paper leaf soap; fold up scissors, kajal and kum kum.

The collective gift was a beautiful yellow silk crepe scarf with small gold sequined paisleys embroidered all over it. I felt so spoilt and wore both the feeling and the scarf with my purple salwar kameez. This day our destination was to be the Taj Mahal. What a birthday present!

After meditation we boarded the buses and stopped for a scrumptious breakfast that we ate at tables outside a Sahaja yogi's restaurant. Tables were now a novelty after living camp style in India. After breakfast we travelled for hours to visit the Red Fort. I had never heard of this place so I soaked up its history told by our guide. It was built with the intent that all great religions were accepted and practised here. A column inside was decorated in bands representing each major religion-Hindu, Christian, Muslim, Jain.

A harem was kept there. The palace was built for games of hide- and- seek with many doors and passages. In the courtyard, Parcheesi was once played with women dancing the movements. There was a special place for the astrologer. His little castle like building was decorated with a Shri Ganesha design of elephants. It was a beautiful place.

After this marvel, we travelled on to the Taj Mahal. The most incredible sight of purity emerged from the thick smog. It was the white marble of the Taj Mahal and an absolutely beautiful river even though it was silted over from pollution. It is said that Shri Krishna swam and played his tricks there. This is all I recall about that day. It was a day swimming in absolute beauty. I had no idea that all this was nothing compared to the gift that was in store for me.

It came without wrapping. It came without me even knowing it and it was sacred. It came in meditation with Nupur, without noticing either the wanting or receiving of it. She came the next morning with small gifts for Tanaya and me. She was on her way to the tailor and took me with her. The mode of transport was my most challenging yet. It was a rickshaw complete with a rapid pedalling Indian man. The cart was on a slope so I had to exert a firm push so that I didn't slide off our seat. I may not have reminded you lately but fear of traffic and possible accidents always rated very highly on my nightmare topics.

Despite feeling very precarious physically, I actually felt secure. We enjoyed the trip but now I was feeling guilty because Nupur was being so good to me and I felt unworthy. By the time we returned my ankle was painful. Guilt had done it again. There was no other description for it.

Nupur did what any true yogini would do. She armed herself with a four candles and a box of matches and headed me into our little hut to find a photo of Shri Mataji. She wanted to give me vibrations, not to fix the problem but to simply remove it. I will be completely honest and say that I did not believe that this would be possible. I believed that Nupur may relieve the pain but I certainly did not believe or even consider that she could remove it. I was wrong. It didn't matter how impossible this concept may be, it was simply achievable. Nupur proved that.

We sat cross legged on the ground and she placed three candles around me which popped flared and spat. She used the fourth candle to work on me by moving the candle in a small circular movements around all the chakras on the left side of my back as well as running it up and down that left side for around one hour. She didn't stop until she had felt she had cleared my left side, especially the Vishuddhi chakra. Occasionally, she would ask me if the pain had eased and by what percentage. Each time I could answer yes and give her a higher percentage. Nupur would not stop using the candle on me, even when I said my ankle felt eighty percent better. I could not believe what I was experiencing and every now and then this thought of disbelief tried to interfere with the depth of this meditation. I forced it away every time and lifted my attention to that place on top of my head that connected me to that other dimension

She cleared it so that my ankle pain simply vanished. Even when we had to go outside to eat she kept her attention on clearing my Vishuddhi chakra. She did this by keeping her attention on me with her left hand palm upwards on her lap and her right hand dropped to the ground. While I ate my meal she did what all the specialists in Macquarie Street had failed to do.

She truly cured me.

There was no pain and no flashing torches of probing doctors coming for their midnight feed of the wonders of surgery. All I felt was a strange whirring sensation in my ankles and feet that seemed to be sucking something out of them, through the soles of my bare feet into the ground. Nupur didn't even realise what she had done. She only shifted her attention from my ankle when it was time for us to get ready for that night's program.

I went to wear my shoes complete with orthotics. I slipped them on but they didn't feel like a glove anymore. They felt bumpy and very uncomfortable. I could not even walk in them. The bus was ready to leave so quickly and without thinking, I went and got the toe sandals I had tentatively bought at the beginning of the tour. I had bought them not to wear but because they reminded me my old hippy sandals and I thought I could maybe just wear them to sit and watch a concert at our camp. Now they felt as though I had worn them forever. I raced off oblivious to what had occurred or the significance of the discomfort that I had felt in my old shoes.

Neither one of us knew what had occurred as I sped off to the bus waiting to weave us through another village to the next program. I didn't even think about it on the bus and that is the truth.

I was more amazed by the thousands of people that attended that program and the artistic atmosphere our brothers and sisters from this "developing" nation had created than by the fact I could now wear different shoes, even if it did indicate a very real, modern day miracle. I still don't even believe that I didn't scream with joy and tell everyone and anyone that would listen. I swear I didn't because in this land of the spirit you were eternally in the present. I felt that everyone was experiencing his or her own personal miracles and didn't need to hear about mine. I think I was also in shock! When my hero had told me I would end up in a wheel chair I had just resigned myself to that fact and felt grateful for the time that I was able to walk. I never imagined that the fate of my legs would or could ever change again, even though I knew that miracles were an absolute reality.

Chapter 24

A Place of Patience

Our last night in Delhi was a smorgasbord of all the contradictions, beauty, and colour that we had experienced since we arrived. Dancers from Punjab, wearing colourful turbans from which emerged a proud plume, completed magical dances of pure gymnastic standards. One man twirled around with another man on his shoulders and another wrapped around his waist with his head hanging down. He was a human centrifuge!

This was followed by an unforgettable performance of a raga by Debu Chaudri. The ancient notes of the sitar and tabla gave a flood of vibrations that made me a very special connection to the earth I sat on.

Our Delhi brothers and sisters gave us one last present. It was a copper badge showing the emblem of Vishwa Nirmala Dharma which means pure universal truth which is the essence of Sahaja Yoga.

We left in the morning and our newly found family lined the street to wave us goodbye after giving each of us the fragrant white flower of Krishna. The journey was filled with mysterious stops- some to have visas checked; some for our drivers to eat and once to pay their taxes. These stops became writing periods or meditation sessions to the heavenly songs sung by Lakshmi.

The bus sped through Haryana. The scenery was very different to Delhi. There were no slums and no heavy traffic. We spent a long time lost and weaving our way out of a maze of lanes before we reached the venue.

At the end of the program our bus drivers who worked under completely different rules to any we could imagine, were in a dispute. Due to a misunderstanding our drivers had not received their meals. They hadn't eaten all day for that matter. We had another two and a half hour journey before we reached our destination and home for the next few days. The thought of all that anger and hunger continuing was very hard for anyone to witness.

All of us were giving very rapid bandhans so that these men would have their tummies satisfied and we would return safely, rather than at a hunger fuelled speed. The bandhans worked but we waited another hour at a border for all these men to argue again. This time it was about their road taxes. Pradeep, an Indian yogi I had met in Delhi had told me that India is the place where you learn patience.

I could see what he meant.

Hours later than expected, the buses finally stopped at Yamunagar and what a welcome we received. This was the early nineties a time before mobile phones were common and we were in a remote part of India so I doubt if anyone would have had a mobile phone and even if they did there would not be any reception. We stepped off the bus at three in the morning onto a red carpet. Above us were tinsel decorations and small candles lit up statues that lined the carpet all the way to the camp. We were showered with fragrant petals by our brothers and sisters who also lined our path. I felt so humbled by that greeting. I saw my own selfishness and couldn't help but think that if it was Australia and our visitors were this late, all the candles would be burnt out and we would have probably given up waiting and gone to sleep. These people were truly selfless and obviously just waited for us until after three in the morning to serve us our hot supper. I learnt what patience really was that night.

We stayed in a deserted army warehouse on the banks of the Yamuna River for a few days. We were told that this was the river that parted for Shri Krishna to escape death when he was a child.

We were also told that there were cheetahs and tigers in the surrounding jungle.

The pollution had disappeared and now nature took its royal place.

The next morning we bathed and foot soaked in the river. Buffalo and cows wearing bells crossed the river as I was washing off the pollution of Delhi. They were met by the men who waited to take them to graze on the other side. I had felt sick the day we made our first visit to that river, but by the time I was on my way back to the camp I felt one hundred per cent better.

At the end of our day we headed to another program. On the way, we stopped off at a spot that Shri Mataji had visited earlier. She had wanted it to be conserved for Sahaja yoga. It didn't seem like anything special. It was just a sugar cane field like the ones we have in Australia. An old Indian yogi asked us to feel the vibrations of that place. That was when you *felt* what it was. I could even feel that cool breeze blowing on my face. We sat for some time chewing sugar cane and just sitting and staring at this field bathing in vibrations and listening to songs coming from the bus behind us. Eventually we resumed our journey through the jungle that was just like driving up Australia's north coast.

We stopped in a small town and we were served icy cold soft drinks through the bus windows. We were meant to have stopped somewhere else for these drinks and biscuits but we were running late. To save us from being late to the program, the local yogis had decided to meet us on the road with at least our icy cold refreshments.

According to my diary, we did make it to that program on time. Without this scribbled diary written at those bus stops, many memories would be lost. Some are indelibly etched but memories of names and places are too attached to thoughts and that was one thing I didn't have time for, as each moment was ready to bathe us all in those amazing vibrations, in totally unfamiliar surroundings, which took me each time to that ancient childhood place of being nothing yet apart of everything and being everywhere.

Now, back to the program. The program, somewhere in Yamunagar was not as full as others and many people seemed to leave before getting their realisation but the vibrations were yet again incredibly strong. When Shri Mataji blew across her hand, I felt it just as strongly on mine.

Those vibrations carried me home and put me to sleep early that night. This heavenly slumber even continued through morning meditation. I made it just in time for the morning meeting. This was a ritual on tour as we all had to know what was planned for the day. After a shoe beat and breakfast we went for a beautiful walk through the jungle down to the river for a foot soak and a splash about. No buffalo joined us on that walk. Instead army vehicles were moving ominously along the serene bank.

After our walk we had a very strong puja, Shri Mataji was not there but the vibrations were so strong. I melted into that blissful state of thoughtless awareness - *that* ancient feeling of childhood. I learnt that in India it is called nirvachara.

We had lunch after the puja and in typical Sahaja style where time can become meaningless, we went for a walk to watch the sunset over that beautiful river. When we came home Sophie and I exchanged vibrations and then watched the monkeys playing on the roof. They were so cheeky. I thought of how much Tanaya would love to see them. They woke us up every morning by running across the roof. They also liked to copy the coughs that some of us had and when they were tired of us taking photos of them, they pelted small stones down at the photographers.

That night we were entertained by more dancers who later attempted to teach the western men these dance steps. The organiser of our Aussie tour joined in the dancing. Later he told us that this was a miracle as he had suffered from a leg problems and had been cured enough to walk but until that night he couldn't dance. It still did not occur to me to make an announcement about my cure.

When I read this part of my diary, I realise that I was definitely in another head space to anything that I had experienced before. Surely, the fact that I could now walk in perfect balance, wearing toe thongs and no orthotics, would have made it impossible for me not to rave on about it and tell how it felt to walk so freely without those clunky orthotics and shoes , but it still hardly rated a mention. Instead I stayed in the eternal present in which there was no cure and no crippled child or disabled adult. Instead there was the true me- healed, joyful, no longer fearful and literally staying balanced.

Given what was in store on that tour it was a miracle that the nervous, anxiety-driven Lisa that left Australia, survived it without becoming a sobbing frightened wreck. It was very obvious that the old Lisa had been lost somewhere between the Qutab Minar and Nupur's candle treatment.

Chapter 25

A Curfew, A Sugar Cane Field and the Lap of the Himalayas

I was certainly shown that this Lisa was so different to the one that had landed in India just a few weeks ago, when idyllic India was transformed into a state of emergency as Hindus and Muslims rioted in the streets. We were all blissfully unaware of the political unrest until it was announced after a beautiful morning spent listening to Sahaja experiences from Taiwan, Malaysia, Brazil, Columbia, Turkey, Russia, and Romania. As soon as these stories ended the announcement was made. There was a curfew in place. We were allowed to visit our beloved Yamuna River one last time, but security guards had to go with us.

Once again we saw army vehicles drive by as we foot soaked in the river and police were stationed at our gate. The new improved me calmly wrote in the diary, "We are all in Mother's bandhan, so we are all protected."

Before Sahaja I vowed I would never fly and I didn't want to go to other countries because I was afraid of things like this happening. Here I was living through the dreaded incident and I did not even realise it. Instead I saw it as a drama in which I had a minor role and there would be a guaranteed happy ending.

We were allowed to go to the public program that Shri Mataji had arranged that day in a nearby village. People only began to arrive when we all began to sing. Shri Mataji was not there and it was daylight, so we couldn't use any films of her talks. The organisers were a bit uncertain about giving the program without one of Shri Mataji's films, but they went on with it anyway. An Indian yogi took everyone through the self realisation process.

Fifteen hundred people got their realisation that day and one young Indian man came up to us to tell us that for years he had suffered pain in his left arm but through the program the pain had disappeared. He even said that he had visited many doctors that all said they could not help him but now he felt he was cured.

This program proved to everyone there that all of us could give this precious gift of self-realization and people could be healed.

The next thing that happened was even more extraordinary. The program had been held at this little village because it was close to the sugar can field that we had visited. We learnt the reason for Shri Mataji's interest in this field. She had looked in that sugar cane field and found a mound of earth from which grew a large banyan tree. She said that it was very holy ground and that the mound should be dug up because something very special would be found there. She wanted to buy it so that this could be done and a temple be built there as well. When the owners heard this, they sold the field to Sahaja Yoga but they would not let it be dug up as they were afraid that if something was found then they may lose all their land, or that their peaceful existence would be disturbed. They had always known that there was something very special about this place and wanted to leave it as it was. They let us meditate there after the program.

We all began to walk to the field and the vibrations began to get even stronger. Grace said she felt as though we were the apostles and wondered if this was how they felt as they walked around together. I had the same thought as Grace. We were both bubbling with the joy of these incredible vibrations and the incredible thought. We hugged each other and held hands as we walked to this special place.

When we got there the sugar cane that had covered it the day before was gone and colourful mats had been laid everywhere in its place. It looked like a huge patchwork quilt. We all sat down to meditate. Grace and I were at the front. It was silent and the vibrations were even stronger and cooler. Some of us began to sing a soft song about the kundalini as our meditation. I felt my kundalini as powerful as a lightning bolt. It moved slowly but so strongly up my spine till it reached my Sahasrara chakra at the top of my head. Then it felt as though that chakra just burst open and my kundalini poured upwards and then showered back over me in a divine wave. This was a totally new experience. My fontanelle bone actually did feel as if it was a fountain of these vibrations spurting up and showering me. I was experiencing the ancient knowledge of this area of our heads. It was a reality.

As I opened my eyes the villagers, including the old man that had sold Sahaja the land were all standing looking at the mound with their palms outstretched. They too felt the coolness. It was a holy moment.

The villagers then asked us to have a cup of tea with them. This sounded impossible but before we knew it more than four hundred westerners had all been served a cup of tea as from every village dwelling, someone had emerged with full teapots or teacups for all of us to use. I could still feel that fountain of my opened Sahasrara chakra long after we left that place. It even continued as I wrote in my diary that night. I felt so full of serenity, love and comfort not to mention pure joy. I was existing with *that* ancient feeling. It was too blissful to continue to try to describe.

Night brought with it another evening of exotic dancing and heavenly singing. With certain notes struck by heavenly voices, my kundalini would just shoot upwards with even greater strength. We watched a young girl do a snake dance and another incredible dance performed by a lady balancing a large clay pot on her head. She not only danced like this but stepped up to balance on two glasses on a brass dish. Next she rocked on the side of the dish with yet another pot balanced on her head and as if that was not enough she balanced on two upturned blades of two swords held between two bricks by the men. I couldn't believe my eyes but this was India and anything was always possible. The night and our stay there ended with us all dancing to the Noida musicians under the moonlight and the red fairy lights that decorated the surrounding trees.

The next day we were able to travel on to Dehradun in the foothills of the Himalayas. We were told that because of the political situation, we had permission to take a short cut through a wildlife sanctuary to the border. By this time being spared four hours on an Indian bus was a blessing.

When we left for Dehradun we were showered with chrysanthemums through the bus windows by our new brothers and sisters. It brought tears to my eyes. A yogi asked me if it was as

I imagined. I said yes, but these unexpected tokens of love felt like nothing I had imagined but like everything I had craved for since I remembered landing.

I sat next to a German lady on the bus. She had lived in the Himalayas. She told me that Saga Mata is the name of Mount Everest in Nepalese and that it means Great Mother and that where we were waiting at a border stop was near the foothills of the mighty Himalayas. She went on to tell me that they formed that ancient holy symbol of a swastika from the air and that the centre of this swastika is where the kundalini of the earth pierces its Sahasrara. I could hardly believe that the heavenly spectacle before my eyes was Mount Everest in all its glory, never mind ponder on the earth's kundalini. If ever anyone was going to experience that feeling of being everywhere and a part of everything but nothing, it was here. Already the vibrations were building in intensity. They seemed to carry the might and majesty of those incredible mountains into your very being. As my eyes came to terms with this sight, the forms and checks were all complete and curious villagers stood and stared at our buses.

As soon as we entered Dehradun our bus stopped under the first banner that welcomed us and the local Indians boarded our buses to spray us with refreshing perfume. Once again we were showered with fragrant petals. We continued through Dehradun, passing people, staring children waving to us, army barracks and more army places until we came to our sweet little camp in the jungle on a rise overlooking the river. Pendals and small tents were set up for us to sleep in and banners were everywhere welcoming us to the "Lap of the Himalayas, the Sahasrara of the world".

We had a meal as soon as we arrived and then set out to another public program. It was hard going because we were all so exhausted from our long bus ride and those vibrations became even more intense when realisation was given. I was sitting next to Grace who by the end of the program looked like a red mound of clothing as she had melted into sleep and sunk into her red salwar kameez and red shawl.

As soon as we got back to camp we jumped into our little tent. Grace signed off complete with earplugs and hat. Our other camping buddies were Jenny from France, and Chris from New York. Jenny and I stayed awake and talked like schoolgirls except that the conversation was about Sahaja yoga in our home towns, our path to realisation and beyond. It was like the downstairs room gone global. I felt so blessed and truly understood what this word meant as I laid there soaking up the peace and joy that was everywhere and in every fibre of my being. It wasn't even around me it was a part of me. There was no separation. I was a part of everything.

Chapter 26

There is Nothing, Separate So There is Nothing to Fear

Our tent

Meditation was before sunrise and the feeling I had when I drifted to sleep was still within me and growing even stronger as we meditated on each chakra. This new Lisa or should I say the returned, original Lisa could even take a freezing cold shower in our makeshift hessian bathroom. The old me would have never even considered a cold shower and would have insisted on the need for hot water just to function.

Believe it or not I still remember that shower vividly. I felt so free. Life was that ancient feeling. I was standing balanced on two feet just like everyone else but unlike everyone else I was doing it for the first time in India and now in the Himalayas.

My only source of knowledge of these mountains prior to this unbelievable experience was Shirley MacLaine's book, "Out on a Limb," and as wonderful as it sounded, her descriptions of the roads and heights had made me swear I could never come here because as I said I was terrified of heights and another of my re occurring nightmares that didn't arrive until I was a teenager was plunging over a cliff and seeing my legs with all screws protruding shoved up under the dashboard. So real was this dream, it even stopped me from learning to drive until I was in my thirties and got that job. Yet here I was standing with no boots or innersoles, having fearlessly travelled in the same Indian buses on the very same road that I was terrified just to read about. It struck me in a moment just how much had changed for me since that instant that I received my realisation. Imagine if I hadn't chosen to go. I wasn't in that shower for as long as it seems because all these thoughts just came in a second. Everything in life changes in a moment. I felt truly at home that morning. I had found what I had wanted; my spirits home and I hadn't just found *that* feeling. I was living with it.

That day we bathed in the Ganges. It is said that this river is the holiest river in India and that it springs from Lord Shiva's head and so is nothing but pure vibrations. Water obtained anywhere along this sacred Ganges keeps fresh indefinitely and will not show any signs of stagnation. Is this because of these vibrations? Rishikesh was the most popular spot along this river but it wasn't our destination. We were going to an isolated spot further up the mountains and not where the masses bathed and buried their dead as western hippies attempted some understanding by gingerly wading in the crowded river.

We drove on into the jungle which kept reminding me of our Australian bush. It even had eucalyptus trees. We had been told that we might see tigers, or elephants. When we found ourselves bogged in the sand with the only option being to get off our bus whilst the men pushed and we said mantras, I quickly curbed my desire to see the majestic tiger until we were safely on the bus once more. Careful what you wish for had a whole new meaning now! We got on our way once more without road service or tow trucks just brute force, bandhans and mantras. Considering our driver kept revving to get out of the sand and that the tyres were almost completely buried, this was a miracle by anyone's terms.

We passed few people, so two women wearing red saris and white bangles that went almost the entire length of their arms, made a striking scene. The jungle was pure and primordial. I melted into its beauty until we were stopped at a check point to be told that the road was too narrow for the buses to be able to safely turn to make the return journey.

I could not believe that my old fear of heights and the nightmare of plummeting over the edge of a cliff didn't make me scream and jump off the bus when I heard the official's concerns. I just felt a momentary twinge of doubt as to the wisdom in the official allowing our local bus boy to convince him that he knew a spot that would be wide enough for us to turn. A moment of doubt and terror flickered in my mind when we began cheering the official's change of heart, as our bus started off on the last leg of our ascent, with a tantalizing view of the most amazing river I have ever laid eyes on- the Ganges. No childhood or teenage nightmares or fears could remain for more than an instant in this person, Lisa. She was completely free and almost literally on top of the world.

We were one of the last buses to arrive at our bathing spot. We could see other drivers stopping to let off their passengers before they attempted the tricky business of turning the bus for the return trip. Our bus driver didn't stop but chose to keep us on the bus for the dreaded u turn. The old fears tried to flood back but I chose to see this as a test of confidence.

I passed with flying colours, considering that when I looked at Grace, she was furiously giving bandhans saying, "Well if a bus full of yogis is meant to fall into the Ganges, so be it!"

Just as she uttered these words the turn was complete and before we knew it we were being served boxes of delicious cakes and savories by the yogis from this destination. We were always so late but our patient hosts checked vibrations to find out our arrival time.

This was the first time the reality of my cure was tested. To get down to our swimming place we had to climb down a steep, rugged track. Normally I would have to go down like a crab to even attempt to get there or I would just insist I preferred to look at everyone else having fun from the top of the track. This time I looked down at beautiful twinkling jade waters of this river surrounded by huge boulders and snow white sand knowing that I could actually walk with dignity to reach it. As I began the walk I was struck with the realisation that the scene I had looked down on was the one from the dream with my mother. In that dream Shri Mataji had shown me how to cure my ankle and now that cure was complete. This was the walk of my life and when I got to those clear fresh waters, people screamed as they plunged into the icy water. I bathed in my sari as did some others. I couldn't believe that I had actually made it into the water just like everyone else for the first time in my life and what a time it was. The jade water seemed to pulsate with vibrations. We took photos and then helped each other to change.

In the Ganges

A little way up the track we were served hot spicy chai and a delicious meal of chicken, rice and yoghurt cooked in big pots on a fire right there on the banks of the Ganges!

We were so spoiled everywhere we went. I had come from feeling empty and without a true home for my spirit to feeling nothing but love overflowing in my existence everywhere I went. This was happening to every one of the four hundred odd westerners from over forty different nations that would never usually have anything in common except humanness.

On 11th December we were to leave for Delhi to catch the train on to Jaipur. This never happened. Riots had broken out in India and already hundreds had been killed including a policeman. Curfews were in place and no one was to leave the camp as it was too dangerous, so instead we travelled further up into the Himalayas to Mussourie. Once again the higher our old bus climbed the more I was exhilarated without even a whisper of fear. Not even the thought of rioting murderers fazed me. I knew I was a long way away from them, but the old me would have had "them" hunting us down to include us in their violence. Nothing entered my mind but the joy of whatever was happening now. When you begin to exist with that feeling of being a part of everything and everywhere there is nothing separate so there is nothing to fear. I was truly witnessing.

We had nearly reached Mussourie when our bus got a flat tyre. I felt that the new me was truly being tested at that point. It was beginning to seem as though the leg cure came at a cost of passing true tests of courage that forced me to face every one of my hidden, deep seated terrors. This flat tyre tested everything- thoughtlessness, doubtless awareness and witnessing, all the essentials of being the ideal yogi. I am happy to say I passed, again.

As our flat tyre disintegrated and the scream of metal could be heard as well as sparks being seen coming from the wheel, we came to the a rest area which was the only spot that was wide enough for the bus to safely stop on this narrow, winding, steep road to the rooftop of the world. Our driver first ordered us all to move to the front of the bus and then frantically told us to get off as quickly as possible because he couldn't find a rock big enough to prevent our bus from rolling back down the steep incline. It was very funny. We all did as we were told and again I was shown that the old me had vanished and instead I was as cool as a cucumber even though that sound of screaming metal had literally been the sound of my old nightmare.

The tyre was repaired and we made our way to the top of a mountain or hill by Himalayan standards. On the way we saw a town built right on the very edge of the mountain. It was actually a part of the cliff face in parts. How this had been built baffled me.

When the bus stopped near the top, we walked passed ruins where English explorers had lived while they researched the area. We kept walking until we reached the very top. In the distance all around us were snowcapped mountains and magnificent hills. Nature choreographed the most spectacular changes in scenery from feather like clouds, to brilliant sunshine as we sat on the edge of this mountain and ate our lunch, and then as we prepared to leave we saw brilliant white sunlight of Shangri la. Finally the sun began to set in soft golden and pink hues. The sun shone so brilliantly on those sun capped peaks. I felt so light and clear and free, so close to all the heavens.

Mussourie

Everyone stayed silent for longer as we made our way back to the buses.

Our departure was delayed until after dark because glass was missing from some of the windows at the back of our bus. The men that had been sitting at the back did not want to freeze on the way home. They insisted on trying to cover them with cardboard and tape which took a long time to materialise. They were successful in sealing the windows but this earnt us quite a hair raising trip back down that mountain.

We were now last in the line of buses taking us home. Our bus driver had a reputation of always arriving first and he was very upset that he seemed doomed to lose it. Rather than allowing that to happen, he just drove down those steep roads in third gear and overtook everything from trucks to our fellow travellers until we made it back to the lead position in our convoy of buses. It was scary apparently but I was literally enjoying the drama, having absolute faith in the power of a bandhan, that weird thing that I had initially scoffed at. It worked because I was able to stay calm and just literally enjoy the ride seeing it for what it was- another chance to see if the old me had truly gone and the new Lisa would stay proudly standing. Some yogis that I had admired at the start of this tour were sobbing in fear; some were throwing up out of opened bus windows and others were just quietly panicking.

At one point we did narrowly miss a truck coming in the other direction as the roads were barely wide enough for one vehicle never mind a crazy bus driver widely passing a truck. We even sped past tents on the side of the road that glowed with fires where no doubt a meal was being cooked for the family huddled inside. By now the temperature had dropped radically. To realize that this was a family home for these people made it very clear that no matter how hard done by we *think* we are at home we do not even know the meaning of hardship. The term "first world problems" hadn't been invented yet.

When we finally met up with the others at our camp we had a hot cup of ginger tea and heard the news that we able to leave Dehradun the following day with an army escort.

DECEMBER 6, 1992: The night after Hindu zealots smashed the domes of the Babri Mosque, soldiers stand in silent witness.

Newspaper headlines

Chapter 27

Riots and an Idyllic Existence

After a cold night's sleep we packed, took photos and set off for our next adventure. For me it would be the test of facing my worst fear of being caught up in fighting of any kind, never mind one that reminded me of war. Our Indian hosts farewelled us by lining the road, waving and singing bhajans. We stopped soon after leaving, to write down our names, and ages for government officials to keep track of us and then our armed army escort arrived.

We had lunch on the side of the road that ran through endless sugar cane fields. It was funny to see four hundred of us with our army escort all sitting in a sea of sugar cane husks eating lunch from our boxes. We set off once more in brilliant sunshine only to be stopped again as not all buses had made it through the check points. This was because an Australian woman who was married and living in India had to rejoin us as it was too dangerous for her to return to her home town in Calcutta where one hundred people had been killed. Her husband and his family were confined to the house for at least two days without any food other than the bag of rice that his mother always insisted was in the house. They were hiding local Muslim women from off the street. All together one thousand people had been killed since the riots had begun. This was difficult for the mind to juggle as at the same time as this hell was happening, we had experienced an idyllic existence totally oblivious to anything except our heavenly state. It was yet another example of the dramatic contrasts of India.

That journey was eerie as we sped through towns that had bustled with so much activity that it was almost impossible to crawl through, on our initial journey. It had taken up to two hours to get through them but when we left, we zoomed through deserted ghost towns with the army on every corner with weapons ready at their sides. Sometimes you got a flash of twinkling eyes peering from the bordered up windows. I felt as though I was in a movie. Lakshmi told me that the riots were between the Muslims and Hindus who were arguing over Rama's birth place and the temple that had stood there until now. When the Muslim king was ruler he had the mosque built on this holy Hindu site. This was done in the 1400's. Since then the Hindus had been arguing with the Muslims because they did not believe that Rama's birth place should be the site of a mosque. This was the first time I learnt exactly what Helja had meant when advising me about wearing bindis and headscarves.

The Hindus had finally "pulled it down whilst we were in Dehradun," as one yogi put it. I only learnt when we got home that pulling it down actually meant burning it to the ground. This destruction had ignited angry rioting all over India. This was why there were curfews and the life of these villages had been turned off. It seemed that the past idealism of all religions existing in harmony had been forgotten for now at least.

Our trip was fast and surreal. We got lost in Delhi traffic and the same passengers that had panicked at our bus drivers speed, cheered as this time he sped through Delhi traffic in record time to catch up with the others at the train station. The men formed a human chain and moved our luggage from one platform to the next, and once again our Indian brothers and sisters appeared carrying large pots, plates, cutlery and anything else needed for a feast, across the platform to begin to serve us our meals including sweets whilst we sat on our bags waiting for the train.

We boarded the rickety crammed train that would take us to Vashi for a couple of days before reaching Ganapatapule for Christmas. I had a top bunk that was exactly as long and wide as me. A pile of luggage occupied the bottom bunk. It was luxury to be in the one place for longer than a few hours. It gave us all time to mend our clothes, pamper ourselves a little and some of the ladies even did their nails.

We ate meals on deserted railway station platforms, in small country villages. The train trip was a scenic movie of country scenes that could have been in Australia with rolling hills of dry grass and no one to see for miles until bright sari clad women walking with their children close by would remind me that I was still in this other world.

As the second night fell, we were told to be sure to keep all window shutters closed and locked as we would be stopping in towns where people were still fighting and there was a possibility that we could become hostages if they realized that it was a train filled with westerners. During that night, I felt the carriage shaking with people shouting and banging on it at one stop that we made but once again this new me didn't even open an eyelid. I just stayed thoughtless until the train moved on and then continued a blissful sleep.

I woke up at 7 00 am on the outskirts of Bombay. We crossed a mighty river and then there was the city. I was expecting horrific sights and smells but it was pleasant. The same production line of men removed our luggage and we walked in brilliant sunshine through clean, calm morning air amongst the locals who were going off to work. It could have been Sydney except for the occasional traditionally clad person. As we set off for Vashi, I noticed a banner above a building that read, "When religion turns into politics, God goes further." This country always remained respectful of God no matter what the circumstance.

The trip to Vashi took an hour. On the outskirts of Bombay were slums that went as far as the eye could see. Homes made from cardboard boxes or scraps of other kind were built in amongst stagnate water and huge power lines-another reminder not to complain when back at home.

Chapter 28

Vashi, a Movie, Theatre and a Victory Ride

Vashi was a sleepy little village at the foot of steep hills. When we arrived at the ashram we were each given a rose and a bindi and our wrists were lovingly dabbed with sweet sandalwood oil. There was a stunning mosaic of the tree of life representing our subtle system made from tiny diamond shaped mirrors in the entrance. The ashram was a two storey building. The ladies stayed in three large rooms upstairs. A balcony ran around the building and overlooked a courtyard with a stage below. The brickwork was extremely ornate. There was also a huge sunroof.

That night we walked around the village of Vashi. Sophie, Grace and I bought identical pairs of burgundy leather toe sandals. This gave me so much girlie delight as I had never in my life been able to buy the same footwear as any other friend, as no friend ever wanted to buy semi orthopedic footwear.

It was only when I walked somewhere uneven or bought these sandals that I was reminded of the fact that my legs had actually been one hundred percent cured. You would have thought I would be trying to ring home to tell everyone but it never entered my mind. Even when the people who were with me and knew what happened encouraged me to tell the group, I would clam up and insist that somehow everyone had these experiences in Sahaja and I didn't want to sound all egotistical making a fuss about it as though I was somehow special. I was almost annoyed at being interrupted from that feeling to even consider it.

The next day we went to the movies to see a Bollywood version of a film similar to "Ghost." By no coincidence, Grace had watched it with her Indian girlfriends before we left Australia. They had translated it as they watched it so Grace knew what was happening. What could have been a real challenge to sit through turned into so much fun with Grace explaining the story line to us. The movie went for three hours and the audience participated sweetly by cheering whenever the goodies beat the badies and whistling when the lights were turned down at one point by mistake. Whenever heroes and heroines were in a chase, the audience would make running movements with their feet while sitting in their chairs, so the chase sounded in the cinema. Audience participation in films was a lot more fun than passively watching as we did back home.

After the movie the three of us talked to a Russian yogi who grew up in Australia and had started Sahaja Yoga in Russia. He even knew where little old Muswellbrook was and was keen to hear all the news about the small programs we had. He astounded me when he told us about the programs he and his wife had held in Russia. He said that there were nineteen thousand yogis in Russia as a result. Sahaja yoga was being taught in schools. Gosplan was replaced by meditation time. Sahaja yoga meditation was being practiced in some offices in the defense departments and the KGB as well as factories. It made what we did in Australia seem feeble. Russia was different, though, because it had been protected from an overdose of religious and spiritual propaganda and hypocrisy by Communism. When Communism fell, Sahaja Yoga was allowed to be introduced. Because people were so keen for these new experiences and Sahaja delivered them, Russians took to Sahaja on a grander scale than anywhere else in the world.

It seemed surreal to be having a conversation of this depth about a country that had been for most of my life the enemy in the Cold War, outside a cinema with a Russian Aussie that knew Muswellbrook.

The next day we were told that Shri Mataji would be coming to Vashi. Everyone sprang into action cleaning everything including our inner selves. When Shri Mataji arrived at the ashram, the vibrations once again built up to an intense peak. We didn't see her but again, I could feel that she was close by. We were told to rest as this is what she was doing. The last thing that I remembered was my head hitting the pillow-quite an achievement for someone whose mind used to prepare lessons in its so called sleep.

After lunch, we made a trip through the slums to an outdoor theatre to see a play. I had associated theatre with wealth so it was ironic and tugged at my heart and witnessing skills, when a little beggar girl knelt down and touched my feet to ask for money. That was the first and only time I felt guilty about the poverty.

This theatre was a part of the oddest multi-functional centre I had ever seen. At one end was the stage which was like a giant verandah of a three storey stone building. The field we sat in to watch this play became a cricket field at the other end with people playing the same game. There were grandstands surrounding three sides of this huge field, just like any western sports field. The theatre was on the fourth side. To the right of the theatre was a wonderfully constructed in- ground, empty swimming pool. India certainly stopped you from believing that you have any idea about the appearance of commonplace things. It must have been too much for my perception because I saw the first act and then snored through the rest of it.

The highlight of our stay in Vashi was a tour to the Elephanta Caves. They were called Elephanta because two huge gold elephants used to guard the entrance to the caves, before the British took them. The caves are on an island out in the Bay of Mumbai.

It would take one hour to reach the Gate of India where we would board a ferry, and then another hour by sea. This trip would make me face the last of my fears. I just knew this would be the worst test of all as I was risking showing our whole group exactly how unbalanced I could be, by screaming my lungs out. I was petrified of deep water because I couldn't swim. I did my best to remain calm.

The first part of this test came when our buses stopped for the men to talk to local yogis who were in a small bay on large motorized rafts. They wanted us to travel in those rafts as they thought it would be more enjoyable to travel by sea along the coast than to drive into Bombay. I was terrified.

When you grow up with legs that just don't work like anyone else's, you avoid deep water literally because you know there is no way on earth that you can swim in it. I yelled inside, "Not this thought" and as I did the men all decided immediately that they didn't consider it to be safe transport for the women. We were allowed to stick to the original plan which was the one hour road trip and the same on the water in a ferry with nice high sides. The men later admitted that they were scared of this scenic coastal voyage too and used the safety of women as an excuse.

We arrived at the bay and as the ferry left the wharf I remember laughing to myself thinking, "Well I used to be afraid of drowning, but now by the look of that rainbow filmed murky water, I'm more afraid of surviving should the unthinkable happen and this ferry go down!"

Before self realisation I would have dived into extreme anxiety but this me just laughed at the thought like a line in a movie. Witnessing powers seemed still intact.

However our big safe ferry had to stop with Elephanta still in the distance as the low tide meant that it couldn't bring us up to the island. There was one small boat waiting to take us the rest of the journey. Another dread of someone who has leg problems is jumping down from anything, especially when you have great hunks of steel and screws in each shin. The chance of jolting it all the wrong way and experiencing excruciating pain always outweighed any chance of even attempting the jump, no matter where it may lead you. In order to reach the oversized row boat we had to jump a long way down, and as people began to do this the boat bobbed around, making the whole idea of jumping terrify me. I remember thinking that this was the moment when the leg miracle would be ripped from me in a ridiculous boating accident. At this point those closest to me blurted out a short version of my leg story and everyone became my legs by saying the appropriate Shri Hanumana mantra and by pure loving non-judgmental support.

When I finally regained not my physical balance which appeared perfect, but my spiritual balance and made a successful jump, everyone applauded me. Once again I had conquered not just a physical disability but that huge paralyzing emotional one of fear. My kundalini or mothering energy that had gotten my two feet planted firmly on the ground was now determined to remove every fear that could literally prevent my journey through life. The little overcrowded boat ride to Elephanta was a victory ride for me.

The caves were at the top of a very steep hill and even steeper stairs led to it. I looked up and smiled remembering how much I had wanted to climb the giant stairway that lead up one of the Three Sisters in the Blue Mountains of Australia but I was never allowed to because I wouldn't make it. Now it was nothing and the destination at the top was far more exciting than the Three Sisters. The stairs were so long and steep that stalls were set up so you could stop and shop for refreshments, souvenirs or jewelry or just to rest.

The caves boggled my mind. They were huge delicate intricate statues of Shiva and whole wall murals carved into each room. The word cave left your mind once you experienced the awe of their interior. As all the entrances to these temples or rooms were around the perimeter of this huge stone at the top of the hill this meant that all the carvings shared a common wall. Somehow the builders knew it was strong enough to cope and they knew exactly at what depth to carve into this rock. It seemed that absolutely anything was possible in India. It also seemed that at this time in history the west was the developing world as I could not think of any mind boggling ancient architecture in my world.

That was our last outing in Vashi.

Chapter 29

A Ganapatapule Christmas with Mary and My True Self

The final destination of that tour was Ganapatapule. It took twelve hours by train through magnificent landforms of huge expanses of flat land studded with dramatic hills and mesas. It reminded me in parts of "Road Runner" territory from childhood cartoons. I never expected to see it in real life. We stopped at another small railway station for dinner and then continued on our way. We arrived in paradise at 5 00am. Ganapatapule is a small remote coastal village. In the village there is a sacred red stone that goes right down to the earth's core. It is called a swyambhu. This swyambhu emits divine vibrations which are recognized by the Hindu faith and so are worshipped. A temple had been built around this one at Ganapatapule.

The Sahaja land was a short drive out of this village. It was set in the Indian bush next to a beautiful long beach where the water always sparkled and felt warm and gentle no matter the size of the waves. We slept when we first arrived and took off to the beach as soon as our eyes opened. We were strictly forbidden from swimming between eleven in the morning and four in the afternoon, as the sun was simply too hot for all of us, even the Aussies.

On our first day we all got together to listen to absolute miracle stories from yogis all over the world. Two were incredible and unforgettable. The first one involved the German woman who had sat next to me on the bus to the Himalayas. Her story would make the best suspense filled, feel-good movie. The German woman had been charged, tried and found guilty of murder without her knowing a thing about this until she was arrested and imprisoned in maximum security for seven years. She studied while she was there and was allowed to leave the prison once for her studies .The two security guards that accompanied her made one stop for them all to have a coffee before she met her lecturer. She was allowed to walk freely and when her guards were distracted; perhaps getting the coffee; this extraordinary woman prayed to be free.

She was seated at a table outside the café. Suddenly a white taxi pulled up and the lady inside called to this woman to get into the cab and she did. Miraculously, she was freed. She fled to Pakistan and from there to the Himalayas where she stayed because they felt like home to her: a feeling we all knew since being there. She married, fell pregnant and then desperately ill.

Doctors told her that she had; forgive me for this image, an intestinal worm the size of a snake which would kill her within a few weeks. She became weaker, yet out of the blue, she craved European food. Her husband carried her to Katmandu where he knew there was one restaurant that served her wish. This restaurant happened to be owned by a Sahaja yogini called Lisalotta, who took one look at this woman and knew her plight. After they had talked to each other for a short time, the woman received her realisation and then for the first time in months, was able to sit up and enjoy a meal. Obviously, she had made a full recovery. Later she returned to Germany where she was again arrested but then, once more miraculously was allowed to go free, as at last a judge saw the truth. These are only the main highlights of her tale.

Now, for the other incredibly unforgettable story about a boy and a tiger. His family practised Sahaja Yoga. The boy was playing in the jungle near his village when he was attacked by a tiger. As it stood over him roaring, the boy called, "Shri Mataji!" and the animal turned and ran away. However the boy still became seriously ill from the injuries that the tiger caused. The father poured vibrated water over his son's injuries. For whatever reason, blue copper sulphate ran from the boy's wounds and he was cured.

My leg miracle was hardly worth remembering, never mind telling, when I heard these stories. I had entered another world where the most fantastic things were possible and not only happened but were becoming a part of everyday experiences. From my leg cure; to rescuing innocent damsels in the worst distress; to saving small children from the jaws of a tiger in the depths of a jungle in India, this new dimension of life appeared to me to be sweeping the world.

We enjoyed many times like this at Ganapatapule, just relaxing and listening to each other all linked by this common thread of Sahaja yoga and more importantly this divine energy of a fourth dimension. We stayed in Ganapatapule for over a week before finishing the tour in Mumbai on New Year's Day. Every day had the same routine. Meditation at six followed by a swim and then breakfast. After lunch we would have some kind of seminar until four when we would all slowly migrate to the beach to swim or simply foot soak and meditate until dark. Everyone would then prepare for dinner and the evenings program which nearly always went way past midnight.

Foot soaking at Ganapatapule

Shri Mataji did not spend much time with us until we reached Ganapatapule. This would have driven me crazy in the beginning as the highlight of these tours was meant to be staying and travelling with her for the entire time. As this was one of the longest tours, I had felt sure I was in for spending the most time ever with her! I should have felt cheated in some way but literally nothing mattered as you were always in the present being a part of everything yet without any effort and hampered by absolutely nothing. Free to feel as if you were everywhere. Free to feel *that* feeling. Her physical absence taught us all an important lesson. This ancient feeling of this fourth dimension did not rely on her being there in person. Of course the experience was made so much stronger when she was with us because she was the source of it all; but she had given us this precious gift that was with us every moment.

When Nupur and I heard that Shri Mataji would arrive in fifteen minutes, we were dripping with salt water fresh from the beach. I decided not to go into panic mode but to remember what all this was about and do it all from the centre in thoughtless awareness. I was ready in plenty of time. Before I knew it I was seated in the crowd that had grown to around four thousand as our Indian yogis had joined us on the tour. I listened to Baba Mama, Shri Mataji's brother, announcing her arrival.

At long last! She arrived in her white car and very slowly walked to the dais. She looked amazing as she just beamed at us throughout the music performance. She told us that the love that she felt coming from us made it difficult for her to speak. She spoke of her visions as to how Sahaja yoga would transform the world. She spoke of ego and jealousy saying that these had no place in Sahaja yoga.

From these high topics she then went to the mundane talking about football. I felt that I was dreaming when I heard those words fall from her lips. I was almost considered un-Australian for how much I disliked this sport in all its forms: league, rugby, union and even soccer. For a split second I dreaded that even Sahaja yoga was not spared from the love of sport, but it past as she almost expressed my inner most sport's thought. She said that we shouldn't become too competitive and aggressive in games and instead take to playing noncompetitive games in the moonlight. She even said that she would write down some of these games and that we should all meet at the beach to play them.

Playing physical games were not just a fear of mine but an absolute hatred. I could never run or achieve any of the goals that were set in any game except the one to become the laughing stock of everyone around me.

Here I was in India, about to face even this, but that thought dissolved as Shri Mataji moved on to more serious subjects such as the rioting in India and pointed out that if people could imbibe Sahaja yoga into their religions then all this would stop.

These were the main points that I remembered of her precious words. It was as if every moment that you were around her, she was working on your chakras pulling them into almost perfect alignment and at the same time sucking any thought or rubbish that may be floating around in your brain.

It was Christmas Eve before we were all summoned to the beach for me to face that last fear of playing games. This time I wasn't facing a fear so much as a pet hate! We were going to have a puja for Christmas that day but it didn't stop Shri Mataji asking us all to play these funny games before anything else happened. She had actually written them down and the Indian yogis were reading from the pages and organizing us into teams.

The first one I was spared from because as great as my new legs were, I still didn't feel confident to hop. It was a truly funny, as in joy giving, game to watch as people had to hop to chase others. The next game was called Coco. A line of people squatted down and crouched into a ball, one person had to chase another. They could weave in and out of the others. The person chasing could tip one of the people in the line and then they had to try to chase them until they got out. There was a clapping game too where people clapped a rhythm, jumped and turned to clap with the person beside them. I don't remember much else about the games we played but I know that for the first time in my life I had great fun playing a running game. How Shri Mataji had managed to get me to attempt this was another miracle in itself.

The puja was powerful and simple. It was of course dedicated to Christ. The chakra that this Christmas puja focused on was the Agnya chakra or the third eye that Gibbo had referred to all those years ago. The main quality of this chakra is forgiveness. Christ had certainly taught this when he forgave those that put him through his agonizing death. Shri Mataji spoke of how Christ's message was lost. She feared that everything he suffered and did was a waste of time. When she spoke of this, I could feel on my vibrations that she had been there as Mother Mary. Now she was here speaking to us. The unbelievable had happened. I was seeing Mary.

She told us that we still had many shortcomings as Sahaja yogis and the example she chose nearly made me choke as it was good old shopping. She reminded us that our attention shouldn't be going there, when we were here in Ganapatapule. At the end, all the Indian yogis queued to give Shri Mataji a flower. It was a bit sad to see people beginning to behave as though they were at a rock concert, pushing each other to get the chance to get close to Her, when all we needed to do was sit where we were and soak up the vibrations.

After the puja I saw an incredible star that was absolutely throbbing. It was a pulsating white light but then changed to blue then green, and then orange intermingled with red and then a violet. I thought that I had conjured it up from my childhood desire to see the star of Bethlehem that shone in that special way described in the bible, so I kept quiet about what I was seeing and listened to others talking around me. They were describing this star too. They had seen exactly the same thing.

We all spent Christmas morning sleeping in, meditating and swimming in the sparkling sea. We enjoyed a music program before lunch. The Aussies got together for a "Christmas lunch". Miraculously cheese, crackers, dried fruits, spearmint leaves, toffees, jams and even vegemite appeared. I could have dived on that plate of crackers and cheese. I always thought I wasn't interested in food but that had changed too. After our get together we enjoyed a rest and another swim in the sparkling water.

Some of the yogis at sunset

As the sun set I walked to the beach. Everyone was there standing in the ocean with palms upturned and outstretched. I stopped and watched. It made an impressive sight because there were hundreds of us. I realised that this was the exact scene in that strange childhood dream of people looking out to sea and not swimming. I had wondered why this dream had stuck with me.

This was what all the twists and turns in my life were all about. They had all led me to this moment when I found that dream in reality. For the first time in my life I was standing solidly on my feet knowing who I truly was and coming to the absolute understanding as to why life had been so chaotic.

Remember I haven't filled you in on all the dramas. I haven't even told you all the ones that occurred on this tour, I have just teased out a single thread that led me through the tatters of my life. All the chaos only occurred whenever I let go of that single thread that elusively appeared trying to show me this other dimension. My life ended up in tatters when I tried to be what I thought I should be. Thought and other people's opinions had made a tangled mess that hid the bigger picture. Through self realisation I was lifted up to see this life in all its beauty and intricacy.

My life was never in tatters. It was always in the process of becoming an intricate piece of delicate lace. I was being led to that feeling from childhood. I had been shown that all those strange dreams and thoughts of childhood and all those early ideas of inner worlds, changing the world and meeting God were in fact the truth. I had been in the hands of the tatter of life that had guided me to find the most precious gem of all- my true self.

I will never forget standing there overwhelmed with this realisation.

This time I had truly landed.

Epilogue

My greatest desire was to share this memoir because we need new stories. It would seem that we have told a lot of stories about what happens on the outside of our beings but not many have been told about our inner beings- or at least not many for the average level headed person to read. We need new stories of universal truth. We need to know about this fourth dimension that is a part of our reality, just waiting for us to connect to it . We need to hear about real practical miracles that happen in this millennium. We need these stories now.

This story happened 26 years ago and to this day I have never had any problems with my legs. I can climb rocks, go bush walking. Miracles are the norm and life is joy. This doesn't mean that life has no ups and downs but it does mean that they don't last and I have the means to *really* sort them out and not get stuck. There are hundreds of people that have a story like this and it's time we shared them so that we can see that this fourth dimension is slowly becoming a part of our everyday existence and that it is a sign of our evolution.

We need these stories now. We need them because fear and confusion seem to be crippling our planet. We don't need anything else to believe in but we do need an experience that can lift us out of our personal, social, political, religious and environmental problems. It may sound impossible but it isn't. Real practical miracles have nothing to do with belonging to any religion. You just need to make your own connection to this energy that is this new dimension.

I chose to write this particular story because so many of us have feelings, experiences and whispers of something more than what we know or see, but none of us feel free to talk about them because often we fear the reactions it would cause. People react for the same reason people stay silent. They are afraid. The truth seems to be that there are very few people that haven't experienced these whispers of something more than we know, but the whispers get lost in the sounds of our high tech modern world. We must rediscover it as it is our next stage in evolution and it is essential if we are to rise above the intricate problems that we are entangled in now.

This fourth dimension gives us access to universal truth. Imagine a world where everyone knew for a fact that we are all one because we all felt it on our fingertips. We all felt the coolness of these vibrations that are talked about in so many religions and cultures. Imagine if all government and world decisions were made by feeling and knowing the absolute truth. If this happened we would truly have solved our seemingly insurmountable global problems because we would all have attained the peace that comes with knowing who we really are. This is how we must evolve.

We all have this mothering energy quietly waiting for us to let it lift us above our thinking so we can see the delicate intricate lacework that is *really* our lives. If you can get your self realisation, connect to this fourth dimension and begin your own journey, experiment, transformation or whatever you want to call it, then you will be a part of this evolution.

If you pass on the book or tell someone else about it then a chain reaction will start. One type of chain reaction has already started with people all over the world who recognized Shri Mataji as a Divine personality within their culture or religion, are teaching Sahaja Yoga but this is not for everyone. You do not have to go to India or to Pujas or any kind of ceremony in order to experience this new dimension to life that I have described in this memoir.

Some of us are not spiritual. Some of us are only interested in scientific proof. Some of us just want to google it. If that's you then google the phrases I have listed at the end of this and see that what I say is the truth. Explore the websites too. The proof is even on YouTube.

Keep an open mind like a scientist. Read pages 111 and 112 again.

Enjoy and begin to know your own super hero…the true you.

To find out more about the reality of this fourth dimension that is Sahaja Yoga.

Google these phrases
- Sahaja Yoga Sunrise (Yes it is the Australian morning news program)
- ADHD research Sahaja Yoga.
- Sahaja Yoga Research and Health Documentary
- Russian Sahaj Yoga Research.
- PubMed - https://www.ncbi.nlm.nih.gov/pubmed/?term=sahaja+yoga Type this in your browser or go to the home page and type Sahaja Yoga in the search bar. You will find 22 research articles printed there.

You will be amazed at how much information is there.
For details of free meditation classes held worldwide visit www.freemeditation.world .
Join me on facebook at "The Tatter of Life" or visit https://www.sweetmogra.com

Cover Photo

The cover photo has captured the fourth dimension that exists all around us. A group of yogis with Shri Mataji was photographed. When the photo was developed this scene appeared. Smartphones and photo shop programs did not exist at this time. This photo was analysed and proven to be authentic. This fourth dimension of universal energy has been captured in many other photos.

Visit www.freemeditation.world to connect to this 4th dimension.

www.ingramcontent.com/pod-product-compliance
Lightning Source LLC
Chambersburg PA
CBHW031109080526
44587CB00011B/901